MW01136021

Control On Leash

Revolutionary Leash Walking Techniques for Dog Owners

By Michelle Huntting

Photo by Amber Craig

Cover Designed by: Victoria Davies

Cover Photos by: Amber Craig

Hair & Makeup: Karen Cribb

Editor: Gayle Davis

Control On Leash

ISBN-13: 978-1480277021
ISBN-10: 1480277029

Disclaimer

This book has been written with the intention of providing information, entertainment and education to pet owners. It is written with the understanding that pet owners will use their judgment or employ a skilled professional dog trainer or animal behaviorist for additional assistance if needed.

This book has been created for educational purposes for both the average pet owner and trainers. Training doesn't come without risks. The author and the contributors to this book will not be held liable for any caused or alleged damage to result directly or indirectly from the information found in this book.

This book has been written as accurately as possible, but there may be mistakes in the content. Michelle Huntting, and other contributors, will have neither liability nor responsibility to any person or entity with respect to any damage caused, any loss or alleged damage to have been caused, directly or indirectly by the information contained in this book.

DEDICATION

This book is dedicated to Lucca, the Spinone Italiano that taught me about leash walking, and to his guardian and my dear friend, Kathy Cooper. Much love to you, Lucca, as you watch over us from above.

Photo by Kathy Cooper

Lucca June 27, 2007 – April 10, 2013

ACKNOWLEDGEMENT

So many years of work have gone into *Control On Leash*. I feel overwhelmed by the number of people that should be thanked and acknowledged for this book.

I want to thank Pat, my first trainer, who encouraged me to become a dog trainer and for being my first teacher in canine. Thank you to the many dogs and owners that have helped contribute to this book. A large thank you to my own dogs (Morgan, Boy, Belle, and Ellie) for allowing me to experiment with different approaches with leash walking. Thank you for all those that helped with photos for this book: Jennifer Caci and Gertie, Miranda Vallade, Amber Craig, Cheryl Kenyon, and Bryan Huntting. Thank you so much to Gayle Davis for your input and editing help. Thank you to my biofeedback coaches for answering my constant questions and for allowing me to take pictures throughout our sessions. Thank you to Natasha and your family for allowing me to visit your farm to learn more about horse handling skills. And, of course, thank you to my parents, Jeff and Cheryl Kenyon, for always believing in me and supporting my big dreams—You know this is just the beginning.

"Be the change you want to see in the world."
~Mahatma Gandhi

CONTENTS

PREFACE

My goal for this book is provide humane leash walking methods, to disprove the myths that we have all believed at some point, and to encourage a strong relationship between you and your dog.

The intended audience for this book is the average pet owner who needs a better understanding of leash walking and for trainers looking for a better way to teach leash walking skills or for a method that works well. It is my hope that all trainers will be able to utilize the methods in this book to better their skills and to help empower pet owners. I further hope that owners and trainers alike find enjoyment in reading the book and using the suggested ideas and methods.

Please note that throughout the book I refer to the masculine gender only. I did this for two reasons. One, I grew up with the traditional English grammar and it is simply more natural for me. Two, it was just easier than dealing with the awkward he/she combo. Know that I am equally supportive of both genders.

Two new and exciting topics of this book are biofeedback and neurotherapy, both of which I believe to be the wave of the future in the field of dog training. In this book I discuss biofeedback and neurotherapy. I am in the process of conducting more research in these areas and look forward to sharing that research with you once it is complete. I truly believe that these areas of study will revolutionize training and change the lives of many dogs.

INTRODUCTION

If you have known me for any length of time, you would know that I am a lover of hounds. Many women go gaga crazy over a baby, but, for me, when I see a Bloodhound, an entirely different side of me comes out words, squeals, and sometimes "baby talk" that I never knew I had in me. I am completely overwhelmed with joy. I love hounds. I have had three of my own so far in my life. Thirty years from now when my current pack has left me and crossed over, I plan to get a full blooded Bloodhound and name him Stanley. If you have ever been around these big nosed, floppy-eared dogs, you know that they love to smell. More often times than not, their nose takes over, and they turn off the rest of the world.

My hound mix Boy and I attended obedience classes together when I first started training as a hobby. In this particular class, we walked around a big show ring in a heel position while the instructor yelled out different commands for us to perform. Well, on our first night of class, Boy and I did about four laps, and during those four laps I never saw Boy's eyes. The only part of Boy's head anatomy visible to me was the top of his wrinkled head. He was drawing in every beautiful scent he could inhale. I remember looking at my instructor after the fourth lap with a look that must have said, "Please help!" because before I said a word, she said, "Michelle, just bring the treat up to your face." So the remainder of that hour, I know I looked ridiculous because I was holding a treat next to my eye attempting to keep Boy's nose targeted toward my face.

My chow mix Morgan was quite the opposite. She didn't care about smells; she cared about other dogs and people. She plowed her way through the entire class time. My arm was about to pop out of the socket. Now, we are able to visit Petsmart® or the vet with some excitement, but maintain focus and ease on the leash. Recently, as we were walking in to our vet appointment at Petsmart®, an older couple was walking in at the same time. I heard the gal say to her partner, "Now that's good leash walking." I smiled at Morgan. We both have worked hard. This is not to say my social butterfly is gone. Quite the opposite. She is crafty and even in a checkout line will often bop her head under the hand of the stranger in front of us. She loves people.

When I would take my Bloodhound Ellie on walks and she saw another dog, she would do a jump and spin while baying as she tried to get to the other dogs. On the second day after I rescued her, a guy in my neighborhood rode his bike by us and said, "Wow, that dog needs some training." "Yes, yes, she does," I replied. After Ellie had been with us for several months, I worked with another trainer (who was involved with Search and Rescue) on passing by another dog without reacting. She was walking on the opposite side of the street, and I was working on different triggers with Ellie. After we finished our training session together and we were discussing different things to work on, she said, "I've never seen a Bloodhound heel before." After she said that, I thought, *Wow she did, didn't she?*

I know what it's like to be frustrated with leash walking. I know how embarrassing it is when your dog is *that* dog. I know what it's like trying to checkout at the pet store or vet office and you are holding three dogs on the leash as you are attempting to make a legible signature on your debit card transaction--- it's not easy.

In 2007, I started on a journey to discover leash walking techniques *that actually worked.* I bought as many books as I could get my hands on to try with my own dogs. Lord knows we tried all of them and were very disappointed. After numerous attempts I finally took a deep breath, looked at my dogs, and knew that we would have to figure this one out together.

I am convinced that polite leash walking is the hardest behavior to establish. I believe the reason for this is because there is nothing natural in a dog's world that can compare to a leash. If I train a dog to sit or lie down on cue, those behaviors happen in their natural world and are fairly easy to establish. However, in their natural world dogs are never attached to a rope or leash.

As I fondly look back upon being a student in my first basic obedience class, I recall that my trainer recommended a prong collar. My spirit tossed and turned over this idea. I am a very sensitive person anyway, but with the trainer's convincing comments, combined with a tired arm from being tugged and pulled, I agreed. The transformation that I saw from my dog in that class was pretty amazing, and I'm still very appreciative of the things that my trainer taught me back then.

On my journey of training with my three large breed dogs, I decided that using a prong collar was still not demonstrating a truly trained dog. I was annoyed by people who jokingly said it was power steering and by people that were content with the fact that without that tool their dog was a bulldozer. As they were talking, I just kept thinking, if my dogs were truly trained, they could focus and maintain a loose leash *without any tool*. But how? What was missing?

I set out on a mission to train my dogs to walk politely on the leash without "power steering" or by use of force. I decided to use what I know about science, motivation and communication. The first day I started this project in 2007, I was working in my home office and would often glance out the window at the people walking their dog in my neighborhood. I smiled as I watched every single owner following his or her dog down the sidewalk. That particular day I remember reading reasons why dogs pull, and the author's response was "because we follow." I laughed a little after observing this relationship from *every* pet owner walking in my neighborhood. Obviously there is more to it (okay a lot more), but it certainly is an element as to why dogs pull. In fact, there are many reasons why dogs pull, and we will cover all those topics and after training exercises that will help in this book.

For those of you puppy owners that are reading this book, kudos to you for training right off the bat and for establishing great behaviors before bad habits begin! Way to go! There is a chapter (14) specifically for puppy activities with the leash that you'll want to be sure to focus on.

Rest assured, I am going to tell you everything you need to know to be successful with leash walking. You still have a bit of work ahead of you, but if you follow the plans in this book, you will be well on your way. Let me show you how to establish polite leash walking with a focused dog using methods that you will enjoy. You will gain a well behaved dog that you will be proud to show off. But first, I want to discuss a few misconceptions about leash walking.

Photo by Dawn Wallace

CHAPTER 1

MISCONCEPTIONS

There are some common misconceptions when it comes to leash walking and the relationship between the human and the dog. I think that once you come to realize the truth, you will not only feel relieved, but you will also be able to start working toward success in leash walking with your dog.

Misconception One: I have heard people say that leash walking is a leadership issue and if the dog is pulling out in front of them, he is demonstrating a pack order, and if the dog is in front, he is "alpha." As I have already said, there is nothing natural about leash walking in a dog's world; so how is it that your dog is walking in front of you makes him dominant in the pack? The idea of alpha is also a misconception which resulted from Dr. L. David Mech's study published in his book, *The Wolf.* Later, Dr. Mech, who conducted the study stated that the idea of "alpha" was never what he meant.

In reference to the term "alpha," Dr. Mech states,

Hopefully it will take fewer than 20 years for the media and the public to fully adopt the correct terminology and thus to once and for all end the outmoded view of the wolf pack as an aggressive assortment of wolves consistently competing with each other to take over the pack.

Also, dogs are not entirely the same as wolves specifically with regard to the pack behavior; and honestly, research is not producing much evidence to back up the idea of the "alpha" dog.

..it is commonly suggested that a desire 'to be dominant' actually drives behavior, especially aggression, in the domestic dog. By contrast, many recent studies of wolf packs have questioned whether there is any direct correspondence between dominance within a relationship and agonistic behavior, and in contrast to wolves, hierarchical social structures have little relationship with reproductive behavior in feral dog packs. Nor do the exchanges of aggressive and submissive behavior in feral dogs, originally published by S. K. Pal and coworkers, fit the pattern predicted from wolf behavior, especially the submissive behavior observed between members of different packs. In the present study of a freely interacting group of neutered male domestic dogs, pairwise relationships were evident, but no overall hierarchy could be detected. ["Dominance in domestic dogs useful construct or bad habit?" by John W. S. Bradshaw, Emily J. Blackwell, Rachel A. Casey]

A more accurate reason for dogs to resist leash walking is that dogs (just like we humans) have an opposition reflex, which means that when they feel pressure applied they instantly resist that pressure. In other words, when the dog feels pressure, the dog's natural physical response is to apply pressure, thus pulling on the leash. This rules out the idea that he is being dominant or taking on a leadership role because science shows us that the dog is innately responding to the pressure his owner is applying to the leash.

Misconception Two: Your dog is being stubborn and corrections are the only way to get him to do what you want. Let's say I hired you to become my office manager and every time the phone rang and you looked at it, I yelled at you without explaining exactly what I wanted you to do. Does that seem fair? Does that seem logical, if I haven't shown you exactly what I want you to do and I correct you for having a natural response to look in a direction of the sound? I feel strongly that with any dog training program it is important to communicate, teach, and show my dog exactly what I want from him in a way that _he_ understands and reinforce that behavior so I see it more often. I believe that good training is fair training. You must teach your dog exactly what you want. Nine times out of ten I notice that dogs are pulling, not because they are being stubborn, but because emotionally they don't have the ability to focus. When the environment is so stimulating, they don't have the ability to calm themselves down to focus on the owner. I think that, even as humans, we can relate. Within the last month I went to a huge American Kennel Club® event, and there were so many people and dogs in the environment that I myself was shutting down at times or just having a hard time focusing on tasks at hand. This pattern happens for dogs as well.

When I see pet owners make corrections with the leash (constantly), my heart goes out to both the pet and the owner. I have learned from science and also from years of observation that there are so many flaws in the practice of constantly correcting a dog. Yes, it is unfair to the dog, but just as importantly, it is ineffective, and the pet owner does not see the desired results. If you continue to do the same thing over and over again, you will continue to get the same results.

Misconception Three: That's the way it's always been so that's the best way. Do you know why heel is on the left side? Walking on the left was based on a soldier holding his gun in his right hand. I am not a dog war historian (although I enjoy learning about this subject), but if you look back at the history of dog training, dogs started being trained to do many tasks for the military during World War I and II. It was after these wars that training dogs became more prominent in the United States. During the wars, soldiers were given dogs to train for specific tasks, and due to the high mortality rate, many dogs needed to be trained very quickly. Methods that would generate very quick results were used. I am not at all down-playing the amazing work the dogs and the soldiers did and still do. However, I think that it's important to recognize that just because it's the way something has always been done doesn't mean that it's the best way or that that particular way will work with every dog. In fact, many dogs couldn't handle the style of training used during the war and were released from the program.

As we progress with animal science, just as we do with medical science, our methods change. The idea of draining someone's blood to help rid the body of a sickness makes us roll our eyes today, but there was a time in history when that was the normal and reasonable practice. Likewise, we can't get stuck on a training idea because it's a method that has always been. It's good to freely propel forward with an open mind. Science is now finally, and thankfully, conducting research with canine behavior. My hope is that in the next 20 years our field will have a large amount of solid research, that people will begin to truly understand these amazing creatures, and that training will continue to evolve based on *their* needs and learning abilities.

I suggest to you this idea: allow yourself the freedom to let go of an old idea to try a new one. Think about the possibilities. This new idea will allow for a reliable behavior, and it will be taught in a way that makes sense to your dog. It will be taught fairly and without harm. I love to let go of old ideas and try new ones. New ideas are exactly what I want to provide for you and your dog through this book. You will learn a great training method that has worked with hundreds of dogs and in the process will build a strong relationship. As you will see in the following chapters, leash walking isn't just about your dog; it's about you too. Your communication skills between you both will grow, and as a result your leash walking skills will greatly improve.

With the methods that I will demonstrate to you, you will be clearly communicating to your dog what you want, reinforcing the desired behavior (thus making it happen often), and also building a strong relationship with your dog in the process.

[Please note: The information contained in this book is not intended to be used as a rehabilitation program (lunging, barking, etc. when on leash). This book is not created for working toward eliminating reactivity, but rather for owners to gain focus and self-control, and build a relationship with their dog while they are working on leash. If your dog is experiencing behaviors that concern you, please contact a qualified trainer or animal behaviorist in your area. Please see chapter 15 for more details on qualified professionals.]

CHAPTER 2

TOOLS OF THE TRADE

As with a toolbox that is currently in your workshop or garage, each tool has something different to offer you. If you need to drive a nail into wood, you wouldn't reach for a saw. In the same way, every leash has something different to offer. The best type of leash depends on your preferences and your dog's response to that "tool."

The Leash
Nylon leashes are flexible and are an excellent tool to communicate with your dog, but there are some drawbacks. Nylon leashes tend to slip through your hand. If you have a dog who pulls, the leash could slip and burn or hurt your hand, especially if the leash is thin. I have seen dogs take off when the owner wasn't paying close attention, and the leash slipped entirely out of the owner's hand. Also, when walking multiple dogs I have found that nylon leashes, which can be difficult to maintain a firm grip on, constantly slip out of position and are very uncomfortable for me.

I do not recommend a chain leash because it is not a good tool with which to communicate with your dog. A chain leash could easily hurt your hands, and it could possibly hurt your dog if his leg were to get wrapped in the leash. I also *do not* recommend flexi leads. The handler does not have the ability to successfully communicate to the dog, and *many* injuries have occurred both to human and dog, even death of a dog because the flexi lead snapped.

My personal preference is a leather leash and it's my number one recommendation because it does not slip, it lasts a long time, and it provides an excellent tool to communicate with the dog. It also works well when walking multiple dogs because it doesn't slip, and I can place the separate leashes in different positions so they don't move, unlike nylon.

Give some thought as to which leash is the right one for you.

The Voice
Every time I talk about the voice with my dog training clients, I think about childhood when my parents loudly called my name versus saying "Michelle," in a softer, lower tone. One voice provoked excitement and the other dread. What have I done now?! Think about how the tones of voices affect us. I believe the expression is, *"It's not what you say, but how you say it."* Voice tones affect humans, and we can see that they also affect dogs. For a moment let's look at things from the dog's perspective. Imagine going to a foreign country where you didn't speak the language. I don't know about you, but one of the things I've done when overseas is listen to the intonation of voice. Even though I had no idea *what* they were saying, I could often tell if someone was frustrated, angry, calm, or relaxed just by their tone of voice. Dogs depend on tone as well. It's important to start becoming aware of the tone of voice that you use with your dog and start maximizing the tool!

Let's take a moment and look at the cue *come.* How do you say *come*? Are there times that you say *come* differently from other times? What about when your dog is in trouble? Remember when I said that if my parents yelled my name, I would rather run into the other room?

The tone of your voice can make your dog excited (sometimes too excited), or it can also be used to calm him down. Higher, faster-pitched voice encourages excitement while the softer, drawn out voice tone would produce a calming effect. Your voice is a huge tool in your handler tool box. Start becoming aware of your voice and your dog's reaction, and adjust accordingly.

Vocal Disrupters

Voice disrupters are something that I am hesitant to bring up with pet owners, but I think it is an important tool to talk about to prevent overuse.

A vocal disrupter is not a punishment but a way of redirecting. I often hear humans use the word "no" with their canine. The problem with this correctional sound is that the dog hears "no" quite frequently in our everyday speech, the result of which is the word "no" no longer stands out to the dog. Dogs can actually start confusing the word with their own name, which I have seen with puppies that get into trouble frequently.

I use the disrupter sound to stop my own dogs from doing something that I don't want them to do. I personally use the sound "eh eh." If I use my vocal disrupter and my dog continues to go towards something I don't want him to, for example, I will then get up and stop him (and later rethink how I can train or change environment to set him up for success). If he stops and looks at me, I praise him and redirect with a different activity. This last part of redirecting is an important element of using this tool. Whatever disrupter sound you choose, be sure to be consistent.

The Marker

One of the method styles I use throughout this book with many training exercises is a marker based teaching method. If you've ever gone to Sea World®, you will see the trainer blow the whistle and then throw a fish. What the trainer is doing is using a marker training method. So when the dolphin, for example, jumps and that's what the trainer wants, the trainer blows the whistle (marks) and then throws a fish (reinforces). I use the same method with dogs. Anything can be used as the marker sound (or, in case of a deaf dog, a hand signal). This can be a specific word (for example; "yep"), a whistle, or most popularly a clicker. A clicker is a small metal strip in a plastic box, which, when you push the button, makes a distinct sound.

For the exercises in this book, specifically, I would encourage you to use a verbal word and a clicker. The reasons are simple: they are the most practical for the exercises that will be conducted. Verbal markers are great when you are on the move (when leash walking) and the clicker is great for really fast behaviors that would physically be easier for you to quickly push the clicker than to mark with your word.

When using a maker method, you mark the desired behavior, and you reinforce the behavior with food, petting, praise, etc.

For example, if you wanted me to sit in a specific chair, you would click the moment my bottom touches the chair, and then you would hand me $50 for sitting.

Because you handed me the $50, the likelihood of my going back to sit in the chair has greatly increased. When you marked my behavior with a click, I knew specifically what you wanted.

With this method you did not use the mark (like pointing a remote and pressing the "on" button) to get a sit. Instead, you used the mark to establish the sit and reinforced it with money. So for dogs we would mark, for example, as soon as his bottom touches the floor to establish a sit and then reinforce with a tasty treat after we click.

Once he is offering the behavior all the time without any prompting, you know that you've established a sit behavior. The next step is to add a name, or what trainers call a cue, to the behavior like the word, "sit." When training puppies, I like to add a non-verbal cue which could be your hand motioning up as you say "sit." After you do this for several days, you will then ask for a sit and see what your dog does. If he sits, great! Mark, treat and praise!

Just as I often hear objections in other areas of dog training, I hear concerns expressed about clicker training. Following is a list of these concerns, and my response to them:

Concern: I will always be walking around with a clicker in my hand. This idea is false. If you use clicker training correctly, you will establish a desired behavior, name it (give it a cue), and then fade the click so that the dog is able to follow the cue without the sound of the click.

Concern: My dog will only work for the food. This is also false. After you start using the clicker and find out how much fun it is and what a reliable method of training it is, you will be addicted and so will your dog. It will become a game to him.

The beauty of using the clicker is it's a hands-off method that helps your dog learn to think on his own. He wants to work for you, and he is excited about doing so. He starts to work, not for the food, but for the sound of the click. The food becomes a bonus.

Just as the clicker is faded, treats will be faded as well. Random reinforcement (food, praise, walk, toy, game, etc), however, is never faded.

Concern: The click cues the dog, so in other words, I click and he sits. I have observed trainers using the clicker as a cue, for example, for the dog to come. This isn't "wrong," but the click is not being used as a marker. A marker is not a cue. A marker is the signal that what my dog just did in that moment is exactly the behavior I wanted.

Concern: My dog will be out of control. Your dog will not be out of control just because you used positive methods. Using positive methods, like clicker training, doesn't mean that you are permissive with your dog. It is important to establish rules, boundaries, and consistency by *always* following through. For example, you have established the rule in your house, that no dogs are allowed on the couch. Your dog jumps up on the couch, and you tell him to get down. He looks at you with those puppy eyes, and how do you respond?

Do you follow through with the rule and walk over to him and help him down? Do you respond by being permissive and allow him to snuggle up with you to watch a movie, just this once? Do you allow your dog to pull on the leash to see someone, just this once? Or do you follow through and make sure that he is walking on a loose leash to a person that he wants to see? *Consistency is a major element to successfully training and controlling your dog.* Using a clicker is merely a positive reinforcement tool.

The "How To" of the Marker Method

Once you have accepted the advantages of clicker training, it is important to next understand the steps in using marker training. I use the word *click* interchangeably with the word *mark*. The steps below can be applied whether you use a word like "yep," whistle, snap of your fingers, or use a clicker. Specifically for leash walking, it is pertinent for you to train with a marker word as there is a lot of movement involved, and it is not always easy for new handlers to hold the clicker and the leash and remember how to move their dog on the leash. For me personally, I have trained with a clicker as well as using the word "yep."

Loading the Marker

Before you actually begin with the clicker training, however, you will want to acclimate your dog to the sound of the clicker by doing what trainers call "loading the clicker." This means that your dog will associate the sound of the click with something wonderful. What you do to load the clicker is click and deliver a treat. When he's finished chewing you will click and deliver another treat. You will do this several times, 6-10 clicks. You will later go back and repeat the steps for loading the marker except that now you will use your verbal marker. So for example, use the word "yep" as my marker. So I will say "yep" and then deliver a treat. I will repeat this several times (6-10).

Now it's time to put clicker training into action.

Michelle's Steps in Clicker Training

1. **Mark (click) the desired behavior.** During this step you choose *one* behavior to mark. For example, if you are working on a "sit," then only click "sit." Do not click a "down," a "watch," or a hand stand. You must only click for a "sit." Clicking other behaviors will lead to confusion. When your dog is easily and quickly offering you the behavior you set out to establish every time, you are ready to move on to the next step. How do you know you've established a behavior? You are in the kitchen cooking when you look at him, and he quickly goes into a "sit," which is what you taught him to do; you are outside pulling weeds, and when you look at him, he goes into a sit, which is what you taught him to do; or before you give him his food bowl, you look at him and he goes into a sit, which, again, is what you taught him to do. You know you have established the behavior that you want.

2. **Name the behavior.** You will still continue marking (click) as in step one, but you will also add the name of the behavior (down, sit, come, etc.). You can say the name of the behavior as he's in position. This, in my opinion, is a more difficult step for the dog because dogs don't easily learn verbal cues. You can, if desired, add non-verbal cues, like hand signals. It is your preference. I encourage my students to use verbal cues because when a guest walks into your house, what do they do? They start chanting "sit" to your dog. The person doesn't know you have a non-verbal hand signal, so teaching a verbal cue, especially for a behavior like sit, will help set your dog up for success.

Nonetheless, a dog's first language is body language. They are so gifted at watching all of our tiny movements, understanding our moods, knowing when we plan to leave the house, and so much more. More than likely, this adept sense plays a role in why it is difficult to train dogs to learn a verbal cue versus a hand signal.

Many times dogs will see a micro movement in our body language and think that's the cue while all along we think they've successfully learned the verbal cue. For example, a friend said to me, "Michelle your son (referring to my dog, Boy) doesn't know how to sit." I replied, "What do you mean, my son doesn't know how to sit? He knows how to sit!" "Fine, stand up straight, put your hands behind your back, and say "sit."" I did just that and Boy continued to stand wagging his tail. I leaned slightly forward and he went into a sit. It's important that we become aware of our own body language, and as the handlers, we go out of our way to ensure that our dog learns the verbal cue. If your dog has learned to sit only when you lean slightly forward, he will not respond to guests that say "sit."

Teach English as a Second Language

Develop good training habits. For instance, when you see your dog move into a down position naturally on his own, say, "Down, good down." Praise him saying, "Good sit," or "Good come," instead of simply saying, "Good boy!" Say the English word as much as possible to help teach the dog your language.

When should you move on to step three? Be sure not to move on too quickly. Say the name with the behavior to gain the association as much as possible, even up to two weeks if necessary. The ultimate test is to say the cue and wait for the response. If your dog performs the behavior quickly, then he has an understanding of the word and you can move on to step three.

3. **Cue the behavior and wait for a response.** Once your dog understands the association of the cue with the behavior, you may continue with step three. For a week, cue the behavior and as soon as it is performed, click the behavior and reinforce with a treat or other reinforcement. During this step you will work on speed (how quickly the dog responds after hearing the cue). Eventually you can start delivering a jackpot for quick responses.

4. **Add stimulus control to the cue.** The wonderful thing about clicker training is that dogs freely offer behaviors. The problem, however, is that if you don't get the cued behavior under stimulus control (only performed when asked), he will continue to offer the behavior in a buffet type style as an attempt to earn a click from you. Do not neglect this step! How do you achieve the desired response only when you want it? You will start to click and reward only when the behavior is performed after the verbal cue. To do this, train in specific formal sessions during step four. If your dog performs a behavior you didn't cue, wait 20-30 seconds and re-cue the behavior; then click for the right response. Once you've worked on stimulus control for several weeks, then you add the behavior to the repertoire of established cues, clicking only the right response to the behaviors you cue.

But He's Scared of the Sound

If your dog is afraid of the sound of the clicker, you can use an I-click which has a softer click, a pen/retractable pencil, or a verbal marker, "yes."

To teach a verbal marker like "yes," you will load the word "yes" just as explained earlier on loading the clicker. You will follow all four steps in training, but instead of clicking, you will mark with "yes" or "yep" as I do. You can use whatever verbal cue you would like. However, I would caution you with using the word "good" or "good boy" as dogs hear those phrases from you all the time. You want the marker to be distinct for him to identify.

More information: I offer a one-hour on-line class on how to successfully use the clicker in training. Please see my website for more details, www.michellehuntting.com.

Above, pictured to the left are box clickers and to the right is an I-click.

Photo by Cheryl Kenyon

Other Tools That Will Be Needed for Training:

- Belt which is described in more detail in chapter 8.
- A treat tote (also known as a bait bag). My favorite has become Premium's® treat pouch. I like this pouch as I can leave it open or shut, and I can quickly move the position of the treat pouch around to have it on my right or left side or behind me. There are many other similar brands available. I used to have one from Outward Hound® that I really enjoyed as well. All of these products can be found at your local pet food store as well as websites like www.amazon or www.sitstay.com

Let's Talk About Treats

Treats are an essential tool to any good training program. They reinforce good behavior and are a pillar in your training program. Later is an entire chapter (7) on reinforcement where you will read in more detail *how* to use this particular tool, for treats are, indeed, a tool. The types of treats that you use during training make a big difference.

The size of the treat matters. You don't want it too big or too small. When choosing a treat, I recommend using a pea size as this size is still large enough that I am not constantly dropping the treat, but small enough that the *dog can quickly swallow*. You don't want your treat so big that he has to stand and chew for several seconds before you move on. If you have a petite breed, and filling up too fast is a concern, you can always use something to lick like a jar of baby food, a Kong® stuffed with peanut butter, or a Lickety Stik®.

The treats need to be desirable to your dog. Imagine if I decided that you were going to work for me for popcorn, and that was your paycheck. So every day you went to work, and I gave you a large bowl of popcorn and, as your boss, felt incredibly generous with how much popcorn I gave you. But the truth is, that popcorn was okay (or maybe you hate it), but bottom line, to you, popcorn was not worth an entire day's work. It's important to think about what your *dog* really enjoys. What's worth *his* time?

Use a variety. Even if you might love M&Ms® (which you would never give your dog), would you love them after having them day after day? I use two to three different types of treats when I am in one fifteen-minute training session. I change those three types of treats every training session. I have about six different kinds of treats on hand for my dog.

Make sure they are healthy. Just like human food, there is junk food in the dog world as well. In the resource chapter of this book Kim Matsko, an animal nutrition consultant, talks about what to look for in treats and she also gives specific brand recommendations. I don't want to give my dogs anything with sugar, food coloring, or artificial flavoring.

Moist or dry treats have their place. I usually have a variety of moist and dry treats when training. When I was doing obedience training with my dog Morgan, I used mostly moist treats. I think that this decision is a preference of both you and your dog.

If your dog is a hard treat taker, then I would recommend using something that he can lick quickly so that your hand is not an accidental target. A jar of baby food, a stuffed Kong® with peanut butter, or a Lickety Stik® will likely satisfy your dog and be easier on your hand. If your dog is biting hard, this could be a sign that he is emotionally elevated and stressed. Doing the impulse control and calming skills in chapter 4 should help with these issues. Also, included in the Resource Chapter (16) is an exercise to help with taking treats softly.

Store bought training treats that Boy gives two paws up:
Tricky Trainers®
Good Dog®
Charlie Bears®
Liver Biscotti®
Buddy Biscuits Soft and Chewy® (also dry)
Nutro Natural Choice Crunchy Treats®

Excellent for petite breeds:
Liver Biscotti Small Bites®
Wet Nose Little Stars®
Lickety Stik®

In addition to store bought treats, real meat is always an option. If Boy and I are preparing for a demo and I am doing many training sessions throughout the day, I tend to use whole cooked chicken or other meats. If I give Boy a large amount of commercial treats, it makes his stomach gassy. Also, if weight gain is a concern, cooked meat seems like a better choice as you can always decrease the kibble (or meals) slightly with the exchange of the meat that will be given during the training sessions.

Other things that Boy enjoys as treats: mozzarella cheese, strawberries, green beans, and blueberries.

Foods that are not safe to give to dogs: raisins, grapes, Macadamia nuts, onions, candy, gum, and chocolate. Please note that this is not a complete list, and it's important to consult with veterinarian or animal nutrition specialist about your pet's diet.

If weight gain is a concern, you can pre-measure cooked meats (or other treats) before training sessions. Some people use their kibble. I still encourage a variety. Please refer to chapter 7 on Reinforcement to gain a better understanding of why kibble is not ideal for training.

CHAPTER 3

KEYS TO LEASH WALKING

Leash walking involves two beings much like a marriage, or even two people dancing the tango. For each of these, we need a partner. A dog that demonstrates poor leash walking skills cannot be blamed solely on just the person or just the dog. It's a team effort. Truly, it is a beautiful thing when both dog and human are able to work together using their own strengths to overcome the other's weakness. How do people successfully stay in a marriage? How do dancer's move together so beautifully? Communication. Without these skills things can get messy. Wouldn't you love walking your dog down the road with ease and grace rather than feeling like a snow plow in Iowa after a heavy snow storm? In this chapter, there are keys and exercises that will help improve the line of communication that I trust will help you begin to understand the "leash tango."

Communication

Leash walking is a two-way street. Communication is currently happening between you, and your dog, but success is a matter of how effectively you are in both understanding and communicating to each other. It is true that what you as the handler are feeling is communicated downward through the leash to your dog. When you feel tense, your dog feels tense. For humans, it's similar to how you feel when your partner or friend is getting worked up and then you start getting more stressed. Dogs are even more sensitive to your emotions than humans. Studying you is your dog's job, so it's important that you always remember to breathe, or as the joke among dog trainers goes, keep your butt cheeks loose!

Communication is not just about your dog paying attention to you; it's about you paying attention to your dog as well. A trainer once told me that my newly rescued Bloodhound and I needed to walk around the house with a leash attached to both of us. I thought this idea was nuts! I wondered what good this would do. How would this allow me to gain the skills and behavior modification that I needed from this dog? But, at the end of the day, I decided to give it a whirl. My Bloodhound and I would stay connected to each other around an hour every day, even when I was watching TV or eating at the table. I had my "ah ha" moment when I was working at my kitchen table. We were tethered together, and I got up to get something off the counter only to come to a quick halt. My Bloodhound was in a deep sleep, rolled up in a ball under the table. I had failed to communicate to my dog so she had no idea that I had moved. There are so many times we, as humans, have high expectations, sometimes even to the point of expecting our dog to read our minds. We think our dog should know what to do even when we fail to communicate exactly what we want the behavior to look like. A good handler is fair, and part of that fairness is to communicate exactly what we want from our dog and when we want it.

In the Moment

Successful leash walking will not come with mindless walking. You have caught me in my greatest weakness. My life, especially in the last seven years or so, has been crazy. So when I finally get to be in the great outdoors, I tend to let my mind wander and daydream, a great way for me to escape the craziness of life with my twins and other aspects of my life. I tend to "get lost" when I am on a walk. When I am with my dogs, however, this is a time that I must be aware and stay in the moment.

The great news is successful leash walking is a wonderful exercise for you to learn exactly how do just that. So, as my friend Karen

Palmer (author of *Dogs are Gifts from God* and *The Secret to Puppy Love*) always says, "Dogs teach us many lessons" and being in the moment is one of them. In order to have great leash walking skills, you must be present and aware.

To further demonstrate the point of the importance of awareness, when I was fourteen, I was enrolled in a summer drivers' education course. I swear that I had the hardest drivers' education teacher ever. In my adolescence I was already a Nervous Nelly, but this teacher would sit in the passenger seat and stare intensely at all of us students while we were driving. I remember feeling drops of sweat at one point. But after that experience, even to this day, I can still feel her sitting in that passenger seat reminding me to be a defensive driver, to be aware of my surroundings. I knew that she was watching my eye movement to see my rhythm if I was checking the rear view mirror and the side mirrors. Learning to be aware of the area around me was difficult. It certainly wasn't a time to let my mind wander. In order to be a defensive driver, I must be aware of all the vehicles and potential environmental changes around me.

From this anecdote, I am not at all suggesting that you must be stressed on a walk with your dog, but nonetheless, you certainly must have your wits about you. The environment changes and sometimes very quickly. A loose dog could round the corner in your direction, a cat could dart across the road, or a flying squirrel could (and quite beautifully) float down. There will be times when you will be walking in a crowd of people. It's important to be aware of the space around you, to be aware of what makes your dog uncomfortable so you can quickly modify the environment for your dog.

Being a defensive leash walking partner and living in the moment is crucial for success. When the leash is on, it's time to forget what bills are due (or past due), the last argument that you had with the kids or wife, or what projects are due at work. Enjoy your dog and stay in the moment.

In the Know with Your Dog

If you've ever had a significant other, you know information about him or her that others aren't privy to. You know before their important presentation at the office that they were up all night sick, their quirks, and things that drive them crazy. As silly as it may sound, you are in a similar relationship with your dog. To demonstrate how dearly many dog owners value their pets, last week I received a magazine that had strollers for dogs and dog carriers that looked similar to the baby carrier I purchased for my twin boys. The reality is that dogs that live with us are in a relationship with us. What I find interesting, however, is the lack of attention, or even misinterpretation to what dogs are comfortable with, what they like, what makes them uncomfortable, what motivates them, and other details that pet owners are really not aware of. Chapter 7 discusses reinforcement, what your dog will work for, so that you will better understand what your dog is communicating.

My challenge to you is to become an observer of your dog. What does he really enjoy? What makes him uncomfortable?

Dogs are Constantly Communicating

I think that it would be pretty neat if dogs were able to verbally communicate with us. However, if they could do so, it might take away the magic of our relationship dynamic. Dogs are amazing creatures, and if you learn how and pay careful attention, you will be able to tell what your dog is saying. As humans, we use our words and tone of voice to communicate to other humans. Dogs, however, use their body. We use our bodies as well, but as humans we rely heavily on verbal communication.

Dogs have emotions similar to ours in that they experience happiness, fear, stress, or discomfort. Although, there is so much research to be done in our field to understanding dog body language, understanding how they communicate will greatly benefit your leash walking training program. There are skills in reading dog body language that will come with practice and time.

Displacement Behaviors

The behaviors dogs communicate which say *I feel uncomfortable right now* are called displacement behaviors. Recently, when I drove into the grocery store parking lot, there was a gal waiting to cross from the store front to the parking lot, so I stopped my van. I watched her as she crossed in front of my van. She reached her hand up to her face and scratched. I realized in that moment that I had stared at her long enough to make her feel uncomfortable. In the context of this situation, she didn't have an itch to scratch; she was feeling uncomfortable. Displacement behaviors are normal, but they happen out of context. Some examples would be if a dog were to shake off (as though shaking off imaginary water), even though he's not wet, or if he were to lick his lips even though there was no food around, or yawns when a person pets him roughly. Displacement behaviors are normal in and of themselves but they happen out of context.

In one of my puppy kindergarten classes, a student complained that her dog kept scratching. She shared with me that she tried a different shampoo, checked for fleas, and made sure her dog was on a good diet, but the puppy was still scratching. I started observing them more carefully to see if I could see what was happening. I noticed that every time the owner cued any behavior the puppy scratched. I explained to the owner that her tone of voice was making her puppy uncomfortable. I encouraged the owner to use a softer tone of voice to cue behavior, and the puppy promptly stopped scratching.

Some Displacement Behaviors:
- Licking the mouth
- Self grooming
- Sniffing the ground
- Scratching
- Turning head to the side
- Shaking off

Photo taken by Renea Dahms

This dog is closing his eyes but he's not sleepy.

Photos by Renea Dahms

On the left the dog is looking concerned, ears are back, and licking lips. The dog to the right is licking lips and turning head away. Both are demonstrating displacement behaviors.

When a pet owner observes these types of behaviors, it's important for the owner to adjust the environment or make the environment look different. This doesn't mean that the dog must be removed from the situation (potentially it could), but it certainly means that the environment needs to be made to look differently to the dog. The owner may need to use his body to block the dog's view point, or if a child is petting the dog in a rough manner, the owner may need to help the child learn to pet in a gentler way. It could mean that the owner needs to gain eye contact with the dog to make him feel comfortable.

If any displacement is observed, adjustments need to be made because the next level for a dog would be stress, another topic which we will discuss. "Listen" to your dog because he is constantly communicating to you; it's really a matter of learning to "see" his language.

Dogs Do Experience Stress
Just like us humans, our dogs experience emotions, one of which is stress. It is very important for you to watch his body language to see displacement behaviors as you are out leash walking because if the environment is not adjusted appropriately, he can become stressed.

Some Stress Behaviors:
- Sweaty paws (You will see prints on the floor.)
- Excessive shedding
- Heavy panting
- Dilated pupils
- Holding one paw up (foot pop)
- Frequent blinking or no blinking at all
- Tension in the eyes or mouth (face)
- Stiff body
- Not able to take food

If you notice signs of stress, please remove your dog immediately from the situation and work toward relaxation. This could be as simple as leaving a park and returning to the car for 15 minutes. You could allow your dog to listen to relaxing music like *Through a Dog's Ear* CD (www.throughadogsear.com), and/or you could incorporate TTouch®. Please see chapter 4 for more information on relaxation.

It's important to be your dog's advocate. Watch his body language and protect him. If you know that he will be uncomfortable, walk away with him. If you observe displacement behavior, then adjust the environment.

Happy Dog
Relaxed and happy dogs will, just like humans, show a softer face and body. You know how tense your muscles get when you are nervous, uncomfortable, or stressed. This is no different for dogs. And when you experience happiness and relaxation, your muscles also relax.

Photo by Renea Dahms

When a dog is relaxed, you will see softness around the eyes, ears, jaw, and overall face. Generally when dogs are happy, they have a nice opened mouth with a gentle pant which shows their rhythm of breathing. If a dog is stressed, his mouth can be closed. What do we do when we are stressed? We hold our breath, and so do dogs. Other times our breathing is heavy. With a happy dog, there is a nice rhythm to the breathing pattern. A happy dog almost looks as though he is smiling. Another sign that your dog is relaxed is if he appears "loosy goosy" with his body. In other words, he is moving around with a "wiggly" body.

Photo by Amber Craig

Also, I think it's worth noting that the tail in and of itself is not a good indicator of the dog's state of emotion. I grew up being taught that if the tail is wagging, the dog is happy. This is not always the case. I have seen dogs with wagging tails attack. It's important to look at the body as a whole. In other words, the tail is stiff as well as the entire body, he is clearly indicating stress. But if the body is stiff and the tail is wagging, I would still assume that there is stress and remove my dog from the environment.

In the Know with Yourself
Besides understanding your dog, it's important to

be real with yourself. My Bloodhound, Ellie, was rescued from a horrible life and came to us with many issues. One of them was with other dogs. So when my Bloodhound was out on a walk and would see another dog, she would begin leaping into the air, twirling, and baying. It was quite the show and one that I would rather not have witnessed. After a year of walking her, I was walking my other three dogs (Boy, Morgan, and Belle), all of which I had raised as puppies but without Ellie. While we were on our walk, a dog came around the corner at least a block away. All three of my dogs started barking, lunging, and generally going bananas. In the moment I thought *Oh my gosh! What is going on?? Why are my dogs reacting to that dog? They've never done this before!?* I realized in that moment that we had, without being consciously aware, a negative association with others because of our experience with Ellie. When I realized what was happening, I started tuning in to my own body. I was holding my breath; I looked down at my hands that were tight on the leash, and sure enough, my muscles were tense. So, because of Ellie's behavior, I had made a negative association and reacted to the appearance of the other dog. This, in turn, alerted my wonderful three dogs that something wasn't right. They were picking up on my body cues and reacting to my tension.

It's important to know yourself. What can you handle? What is too much for you? Self knowledge is part of this journey to understanding and working well with your dog. If you are uncomfortable with greeting the new poodle that's walking past you and your dog, then continue walking. Just as dogs understand non-verbal communication, people do too. If you are uncomfortable with the lunging, yappy dog that's walking down the block, then make a turn or go in the opposite direction. Avoiding potential conflict or stress doesn't make you a "bad" pet owner. It makes you a wise pet owner. I talk all the time throughout my books about setting your dog up for success, but it's also equally important to set yourself up for success. Knowing your limits is a good thing.

It's important to know your body. How are you holding the leash? Did you wrap it seven times around your hand before opening the door to go out on a "relaxing" walk? It's important to check in with your body. How are you breathing? If you are breathing short, shallow breaths, then you are probably stressed. If that happens, then begin to target your breath and make sure that each breath touches the bottom of your lungs before you allow the air to flow back out again. How are your muscles? Where are they tight? Consciously relax them and revisit them while on a walk. Dogs are very sensitive to us and even more sensitive when they are in a relationship with us, so be aware of subtle physical signals you are sending your dog. This is a learning process, obviously, but it truly is an element to consciously be aware of as you take your dog out for a walk.

Space Etiquette

Space means everything in the dog world. Dogs communicate very differently than we do when it comes to space. A good example of this would be with herding breeds. If you have ever watched a dog move the sheep, he will always move *in the direction that he wants the sheep to go.* As a human, if I wanted you to move closer to me, I would begin walking closer to you, and you would understand to move closer to me, whereas if I walked towards a dog, he would more than likely move in the same direction that I was walking, which would be moving away from me. This is why when you run after your dog when he gets loose, he continues to move away. If you ran in the direction that you wanted him to go, he would more than likely begin to follow you. The other major difference in communication with dogs and people is that as humans we use our hands to point and show direction. "Put that chair over there" as we point and move our arm out to the side. A dog doesn't understand a point (unless specifically trained as a cue).

For a dog, space is respected. For example, if Boy were lying in the hallway, Belle would arc completely around him as to avoid his space because at that moment in time he owns it and she respects it. If she didn't respect that space, there is a good chance that Boy would correct her. A good handler is consciously aware of and respects space as he is passing by another dog on a leash. Use your body to avoid any potential "tiffs" with other unknown dogs. Just because someone yells out that his dog is safe, you don't know how yours will respond. I don't encourage interaction with other dogs when I am walking my dogs on the leash. When the leash is on, it's not time to socialize.

Use Your Body

Using your own body to protect your dog is an essential part to great leash walking. In the dog world, we would call you a good handler if you are able to use your body to protect your dog. Here is an excellent example: When Boy and I were at a training conference, we were walking into a room with tight space. There were two dogs that we were going to pass us on our left. I knew that they were friendly dogs, but I wasn't interested in Boy greeting them. So before we got to that area of the room, I quickly switched Boy to my right side and used my own body as a "block" from the other two dogs that we quickly (I made sure to walk fast) passed by in the small space. When you start becoming aware of the environment and aware of a dog's space etiquette, you can successfully use your own body to protect your dog in many different situations.

Using Your Body To Protect Your Dog

Photo by Miranda Vallade

Jennifer sees Michelle and Boy coming and in this particular situation wants to use her body to maintain Gertie's focus.

Photo by Miranda Vallade

Arcing

Arcing is another tool that is very useful when on a walk with your dog. If you come across a group of people or a dog that you know is a little too happy or maybe lunging too much for your comfort, you can use the tool of arcing (or completely turn around to get out of the situation). Arcing is a great tool to keep your dog safe, but also in the dog body language world, arcing is a polite way of saying *I come in peace.*

In the diagram above, as the two dog walkers are approaching one another, the one on the left shifts the dog to his left side, opposite of the side the other dog is on and shortens up on the leash, much as a batter chokes up on a bat, to gain greater control and proximity to my dog. As they briskly move closer the man on the right will start to arc. He says, "Hello" (not to be rude to the other pet owner, but assertive) and he continue moving.

Using Your Body to Protect Your Dog: Arcing

Photo by Miranda Vallade

Michelle (right) has an "excited," unfamiliar dog approaching and is yelling out to Jennifer that her dog wants to say, "Hi." Jennifer doesn't want to interact, so she will arc around Michelle and Boy, who is the role-playing dog. Also note in the picture below that Jennifer switched sides to be a "barrier" between her dog and Boy.

Photo by Miranda Vallade

So what if you *must* pass another dog?

If you must pass another dog in a tight space, then you can use your body as well as other things in the environment, a group of trees for example, to be a block. In the pictures below, Jennifer and I demonstrate how to use our own bodies to provide a block for our dogs. This action simply demonstrates good handling skills and the two of us using good space etiquette. Doing something this simple can make all the difference in the world. Most importantly, if you are ever in a tight environment, this shift very well could keep your dog safe.

Photo by Miranda Vallade

Photo by Miranda Vallade

Photo by Miranda Vallade

Photo by Miranda Vallade

So what if a loose dog approaches?

This is a great question as it happens quite often in our neighborhood. It is quite frustrating, and as a veteran trainer, even I at times have gotten stressed. It's usually from the neighbors with the giant German Shepherds that are dashing straight for me and my family, as the owners are saying, "Don't worry; he's friendly!" And I am yelling back, "But mine's not!!" I knew from the very initial impolite greeting that the meeting of our dogs would not go over well.

Other tips for keeping your dog safe in potentially dangerous situations are as follows:

- At times I've had to use a non-threatening "S" type movement to continually walk my dog around while the neighbor attempted to tether her dog. This seemed to work for us and it was really the best option. Humans walk lateral, but if a dog walks lateral it is considered a threat, so this is why I walk in an "S" type movement to prevent any miscommunication with the loose dog approaching.
- If you are in a situation like a trial, show, or training class, you can send your dog to his crate.
- Sue Sternberg had the great idea of teaching a dog to stick his head between the handler's legs on cue to get treats from behind the handler's back. The idea behind this is to prevent the dog from seeing the loose dog face-to-face while the handler deals with the situation.
- If you have treats on you, as a distraction, when a potentially dangerous dog approaches, you can throw them away from you, and as the dog starts eating them, quickly leave the situation.
- If your dog is small, pick him up and turn your back to the loose dog. This is truly a matter of safety for your little dog.
- If you are very worried about loose dogs, then you can carry an emergency tool to stop a dogfight or to escape without risking an injury (Direct Stop® citronella spray).

Exercises to Help Build Connection & Focus

Connection and focus are key with leash walking. As I have mentioned, leash walking is a lot like dancing with a partner. As you both get to know each other, understand each other's quirks, understand the way each other communicates, you will

be able to come together harmoniously as a team. Just like a dance routine, practice is involved with leash walking. I have put together exercises that will establish, build, and grow communication skills. These are foundational exercises to focus on especially in the beginning phase of training leash walking.

Life Line

Leash your dog to you while you are doing things around the house, even if it is for 30 minutes or so while watching TV. This is an excellent learning opportunity for you and your dog. This exercise will help you work toward great leash walking skills. If you are brave and would like to do this exercise for a longer period of time, go for it! You can also incorporate eye contact into this exercise.

When your dog gives or maintains eye contact, you can add a hand signal like drawing your hand up to the side of your eyes and reward him for the eye contact. You can do this throughout your time on the leash.

You can incorporate this exercise into your everyday life as you are vacuuming, doing dishes, folding laundry, or other chores. While you are doing these activities watch for any eye contact, add your hand signal, and reward. You can also incorporate on a walk.

Remember, when you are working on this exercise, you should not expect a long romantic gaze at first. You can work toward longer looks as you progress in your training. So, in the very beginning stage you may get a fast glance of your dog's eye, and I would reward this. Gradually, as you continue working together, you can expect longer looks from your dog.

Distracted Dog

Take a handful of treats, your clicker, and walk your dog on leash. Every time your dog becomes distracted and then looks toward your vicinity, click, treat, and tell him to go sniff again. Do not wait for a long look; watch for even quick flicks of his eye. You can start this exercise in the backyard. Make the exercise more difficult by moving to the front yard and a new location. With this exercise, there may come a point where you will need to send your dog a distance away from you by saying "go sniff" because he won't stop looking at you. Boy has gotten pretty savvy at this game. I will send him to a location a short distance away from me, and he will pretend to sniff, (not even all the way to the ground), while still looking at me.

Distracted Dog Exercise

Photos by Miranda Vallade

Michelle sends Boy out by saying "go sniff." As soon as Boy looks at her she clicks and he runs to her to get a treat.

Photos by Miranda Vallade

Give a Look, Get a Treat

Once again, take a handful of treats, clicker, and the dog on leash outside, at first preferably on cement. Throw a treat on the ground and tell your dog to "go get it." Watch his eyes, and as soon as you see a glance toward your area, click and throw the next treat, cueing him to "go get it." Repeat until all the treats are gone. Note: The glance can be a very fast motion of the dog's eye toward your face. Do not be picky with this behavior at first. Gradually raise your criteria as you work with this exercise.

Photos by Miranda Vallade

All in All

Communication is the foundation for all training programs especially leash walking. With the quick movement, the unpredictable environment, and the distractions, you must work as a team, constantly communicating and listening. You must know each other so well that together, with both skill and grace, you make immediate adjustments based on the changes in the environment, resulting in polite and controlled leash walking.

"The art of communication is the language of leadership."

— James Humes

CHAPTER 4

CALMING SKILLS & IMPULSE CONTROL

Imagine that you were about to bungee jump, and you were standing on the bridge getting suited up with the help of professionals. How would your body feel at that moment? I have never (nor do I plan to) bungee jump, but I can imagine that my heart would be pounding, my hands sweating, my stomach turning, and there is a good chance that I would need to run to the bathroom. If a friend, who probably was the one that talked me into jumping off a bridge in the first place, was trying to teach me math equations while they were suiting me up, I would not be able to answer her. If she asked me after we jumped what I remembered of what she had taught me, I highly doubt that I would be able to give her any information.

Why would I react in such a way? In this situation my adrenal glands were in emergency situation mode, and I was not in an emotional state for optimal learning. For me, optimal learning happens with lower lighting, soft instrumental music, and someone talking me through a math problem as I work through the problem myself.

It most certainly would not involve jumping off a bridge! Dogs have optimal learning too. As I have observed people (and from my own experience), it seems that we expect dogs to go outdoors where heightened senses occur, and because we are such a great leaders, or so we think, we expect that they will focus. In the meantime, the dog is on sensory overload. They see grasshoppers jumping in the grass, a squirrel jumping from tree to tree, and they smell the road kill from last night. We expect our dog to love or "respect" us so much that he will choose to look up at us, to not pull, and to ignore all else including the very cute poodle that just wagged her tail as she walked by! In my bungee jumping situation, I was not being "disrespectful" to my friend by not being able to focus on what she was teaching me. My body's nerves and adrenal glands, and Lord knows what else, had taken over.

I have a lot of friends that are soldiers and when they prepare for war they are trained and re-trained so it prepares them for highly exciting, adrenal pumping situations. Because of extensive training, the soldiers have learned to think through what they need to do. We can provide a similar experience and training for our dogs. A dog needs to learn self-control and the ability to think through his emotions in exciting situations, but he needs our help to do so!

How can we help them? By using exercises to teach impulse control and calming skills.

Transition Times are Training Times
Before I start explaining the impulse control exercises, it is important to realize that the exercises can be very exciting to a dog, a handler must give an in-between, transition time. I have noticed that we, as humans, do a really great job getting our dogs excited. Often, I hear pet owners share that when the partner comes home from work, the dogs are already excited. There usually is talking in a high pitched voice and running and jumping around the yard with them. After all this excitement the pet owner comes back inside, leaving the dogs outside. That was a perfect example of what not to do if you wish to teach your dog impulse control. The dogs are extremely excited when the owner leaves, so figuratively the dogs got all dressed up with no place to go!

Though there is absolutely nothing wrong with playing and having fun with your dogs, it is important to help them bring themselves back down. From observing the dogs that I've worked with, I have rarely seen a dog that naturally knows how to bring himself back down, so this is something that they need help learning.

What does a transition time look like?

The transition time is a structured time, in which you help bring your dog back down emotionally. This time can come in the form of a relaxed, leashed stroll in the backyard. Chewing also releases endorphins, so giving him a stuffed Kong® or bone while he's lying on his mat or in his kennel is a good transitional activity. A massage with TTouch® can be an excellent way to help a dog calm himself (more information on TTouch® is in Chapter 4).

Please don't expect a dog to be able to do this on his own quickly. You will need to teach him. Every dog is different too. What I do for, Morgan, for example, to help her relax will be different than Boy. Eventually your dog will learn how to bring himself down much easier on his own, but it is up to you as the handler to teach him these skills.

Creating a Pattern

Pattern games create, as their name suggests, a pattern for your dog by getting him excited and then by doing something to bring him down. This creates a wave-like pattern of taking his excitement level up and down. The purpose of this exercise is to help him learn to think through his excitement. Most dogs do not possess this skill. This is part of the reason your dog jumps when encountering new people. Even though your dog knows and understands the cue "sit," during his excitement he continues to jump.

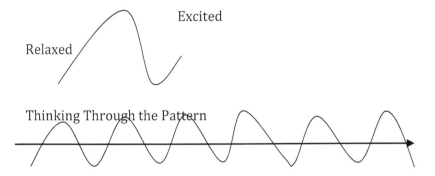

(Another reason for jumping could be he needs more reinforcement for the correct behavior.) It is of key importance for you as the dog's handler to watch the dog as you take him through these exercises. You do not want your dog too excited for too long during the arousal part of the on/off games because the dog could go beyond what he is emotionally able to handle and will not be able to bring himself back down. Again, this would be like getting him dressed up with no place to go. This is not the purpose of the game. Rather, the purpose is to create a pattern within your dog's ability to get him slightly excited and to bring him back down.

What is the relationship between impulse control and leash walking? When dogs are on the leash, there are all sorts of exciting environmental things going on around them including squirrels, people, other dogs (sometimes overly excited dogs), and movement. Teaching your dog to think through his excitability will set him up for success when you are out in the real world.

First exercise: Creating a Wave
Okay, I will forewarn you on this exercise that you will feel a bit silly at times. Don't worry about what the neighbor dogs are thinking! It's okay because the exercise will help your dog. You can start this exercise indoors until your dog has become well focused and will remain in a sit, and then take him to the backyard and then front yard as you both become more confident.

As a handler during this exercise, you have the additional tool of your voice. Using a softer, lower tone can help bring your dog back down emotionally. There will be times in between activities that you will need to stop and use a softer, lower voice to talk to your dog to help calm him. It may be a drawn out, "Goooood boooy." For very excitable dogs, the session may be less than 15 seconds, and the exercise should not be conducted longer than 3 minutes at a time with any dog. I recommend training up to 3 minutes once a day, or doing a couple, 1-to-2 minute sessions per day. The benefit for you will be a focused dog as well as a nice, short cardio work out for yourself.

While you are doing the exercise, it's important to watch your dog's breathing and body language so you don't take him too far up the excitability scale. Any time he gets revved up in the process re-cue a "sit" and talk in a soft, low voice. If you do take your dog over the point of excitability you can leash him and take him on a leisure walk in your backyard for several minutes and then give him something to chew while lying on his mat.

Now you will need a handful of treats and clicker. You should click if your dog stays in a sit position when you do the following exercises. At the end of each exercise, you will click and treat when he's in a sit (or down) position.

a.　Cue your dog to sit.
b.　Act as if you are going to jump (but don't).
c.　Sway side to side.
d.　Jump up once.
e.　Sing.
f.　Clap your hands.
g.　Act as if you are going to jump (but don't).
h.　Roll your tongue making a high-pitched sound.
i.　Move from side to side.
j.　Move your arms around.
k.　Jump up.
l.　Run up towards your dog.
m.　Run in place.
n.　Do jumping jacks.
o.　Sing.

Exercise: Running backwards and cueing "sit" with a look
Again, you will need a handful of treats and clicker for this exercise. Place your handful of treats in front of your dog's nose and make a sound as you run backwards a few steps to encourage him to follow you. Cue a "sit" and come to a stop. As soon as he sits, click and reward with a treat. Continue the game. There are some dogs that may need to sit a bit longer before resuming to the game. When the handful of treats is gone, end the game.

An indication that your dog's excitement level is becoming too elevated and you may need to slow things down occurs when the dog begins taking treats hard. If this happens, you can ask for a longer sit and talk in a slower and lower tone. Another indication is if your dog starts to nip. When this happens, you can pick up the leash and start walking your dog slowly around the yard and end the session. The next session, do not work for such a long period of time.

During the exercise, it's crucial that you pay attention to his small body cues. We want to create a wave-like pattern, but we don't want to create a tidal wave. Over-doing it is not advantageous. It really will take observational skills throughout this exercise to know when to push and when to ease up.

Protocol for Focus & Relaxation

If your dog is extremely excitable, then I would recommend my Protocol for Focus & Relaxation. This protocol was inspired by Dr. Karen Overall's Protocol for Relaxation. I created my own version that I felt specifically focused on creating focus and relaxation for leash walking. This is a 14-day program with exercises to do each day. By creating wave-like patterns, the protocol will reinforce calm behaviors while you are taking your dog through the tasks. The protocol is included in the Resource Chapter (16).

Exercise: Stay

The *stay* cue promotes strong impulse control for your dog and helps him learn to focus. Teaching stay will help with the overall program, but you will also use stay while out walking your dog. You may use a *stand* or *sit-stay* before you cross the street, if you need to tie your shoe, and many other times you find yourself needing a strong stay behavior.

I teach stay a little differently than I originally learned using traditional methods. I prefer to set dogs up for success by not adding the cue first. Rather, I will establish the behavior of *stay* and then add the cue *stay*. This reversal of the traditional order prevents constant corrections. During the process of establishing the *stay* behavior, I will not use the cue *stay*, but I will still use a release cue such as *okay.*

When you first start teaching the behavior of *stay*, you establish the behavior by encouraging duration. Once you've established a 15-second duration, you will start working with distance by having the handler back up.

How you teach stay:

1. Cue your dog to "sit." Click when he sits. Stand by him and give an occasional treat.
2. Once your dog is able to sit with you standing by him for about 15 seconds, then move on to the next step.
3. Start adding movement. Click if your dog stays in a position. Note: If my dog moves into a down instead of a sit, I find this acceptable.
   a. Rock back and forth. If your dog stays in a sit position, click and treat.
   b. Pick your feet up as you rock back and forth. If he stays, click and treat.
   c. Move your feet back and forth in front of dog. If he stays, click and treat.
   d. Pivot your foot back and forth. If he stays, click and treat.
   e. Take one full step to the side then the other side.
   f. Take one full step back.
   g. Take two full steps back.
   h. Take a step to the dog's side. If the dog stays, click and treat.
   i. Step to the dog's other side. If he stays, click and treat.
   j. Walk around the dog while luring him with a treat in front of his nose.
   k. Give your dog your back while you turn your head to maintain eye contact.
   l. Dance in front of your dog.
   m. Talk in a high-pitched voice.
   n. Run up towards your dog.
   o. Sing in front of your dog.

p. Give your dog your back and only look back occasionally to build stay duration.
q. Walk away giving your dog your back, but still look back occasionally.
r. Move halfway around your dog.
s. Shift weight and rock in front of him.
t. Move all the way around the dog.

Once the dog is able to stay while you move, it is time to add the "stay" cue. I verbally cue this, but I also add the non-verbal cue of my hand flat out in front of the dog's face. You will repeat all the steps listed above, but this time you will add the cue.

Photo by Cheryl Kenyon

Importance of the Release Cue

The release cue is very important and often forgotten. It is imperative to communicate to your dog that he has permission to get out of the stay position. When handlers forget to communicate the release cue, dogs are confused or hesitate. Dogs need consistent communication. Be consistent with your release cue no matter what behavior you are releasing because, to your dog, this cue means he will have permission to move around. *Come* is such an important cue and should not be used as a release cue with *stay*. I use *okay* as my release word.

For example, you will cue your dog to "stay," do one of the activities on pervious page, and then say "okay." As you give the release cue, be sure to remain stationary. The reason for this is, if you move as you say "okay," your dog will learn to watch your body movement rather than learning to listen for the verbal cue. If you move and then say the release word, he will more than likely follow your non-verbal cues.

Cue "stay" → Do one of the activities → Cue verbal release → Move

Following the pattern I have suggested will help you set your dog up for success. After you say the release cue "okay," then you should encourage your dog to get up (movement, a kissing sound, snap of fingers, or a hand clap.) Using this method will help your dog to begin associating the behavior of moving out of stay position with your release cue (like "okay").

Photo by Cheryl Kenyon

Michelle said the release word and turned to walk away. Release is not supposed to be exciting, and no treats should be given for the release.

The following pictures demonstrate the stay exercise:

Photo by Cheryl Kenyon

Photo by Cheryl Kenyon

Photo by Cheryl Kenyon

Photo by Cheryl Kenyon

Photo by Cheryl Kenyon

What do you do if your dog breaks out of stay?
First of all, handlers need to use their skill to read the dog and know how long he stays and give a release cue before that point. It is important to set the dog up for success. You don't want to push the dog beyond what he can do within a training session. If the dog has already popped up then go ahead and use the release cue. In the next session, give the release cue for a shorter period in a stay.

4. Once the dog is able to complete all the tasks in the preceding list, with the addition of adding the cue "stay" and a release cue, you will begin to add distractions. Any time we add a higher criteria, we always lower other criteria. You will shorten the duration when adding a distraction and then gradually increase duration with each individual distraction from there. Your dog may be on leash, or dropped leash, during this exercise.

> u. Throw a neutral object up and down.
> v. Have a *known person walk by.
> w. Throw a neutral object up and down.

* A known person is someone that your dog is familiar with.

(A neutral object is an object that your dog doesn't have an emotional response to. For example, the tennis ball would not be a neutral object for Boy because he loves his tennis ball. If, however, I used a remote control, for example, this object has no emotional response from Boy).

    x. Throw a higher level object up and down.

(A higher level object would be an object that means a little more, but not one that would be super exciting. For Boy a tug toy would rank in this level of toy, but a tennis ball would be at the top of the scale.)

    y. Throw a neutral object by your dog.
    z. Have someone ring the door bell and cue a stay. Do not go to the door.
    aa. Throw a higher level object by your dog. (You can have the dog on leash)
    bb. Have someone ring the door bell and cue a stay, walk to door but do not open it.
    cc. Have a known person walk close to your dog.
    dd. Have a known person speak to your dog while walking by.
    ee. Have a known person, without talking, pet your dog.
    ff. Have someone ring the door bell. Cue a "stay," then open and shut door quickly.
    gg. Talk excited to the dog.
    hh. Have known person talk in a normal voice to your dog (no petting).
    ii. Have someone ring the door bell. Cue a "stay," open and shut door, leaving it open longer.
    jj. Have a known person (and possibly a dog) walk by. Start with each handler team on opposite sides of road walking in opposite directions past each other so you are facing each other as you pass. After every pass on the street, each person will take one step closer toward each other before doing another pass. The goal here is to decrease the space between the two groups as they pass each other. Dogs should not interact. If dogs are doing well, you can change to walking parallel, starting with the greatest distance (on

opposite sides of road) and gradually decreasing the space for each pass.

kk. Have a known person and dog come up within 6 feet of the dog, greet both of you quickly, and then walk away.

ll. Have someone ring the door bell. Open the door and talk for one second.

Leave It!

A solid *leave it!* cue will not only promote impulse control and focus but also will be a great tool for you when you are on a walk with your dog. You can use the cue *leave it!* when your dog tries to eat something he shouldn't and also if there are kids or pets your dog wants to interact with during the walk.

This cue will progress to the point where you can throw hot-dogs at your dog's face, and he will leave them alone. How can the dog have such amazing control? You have taught the dog if he leaves it as you have cued, he will get something even better. For example, if I asked you to leave a $50 bill you would say, "No way, Miss Michelle." But if I said, "If you drop that $50 bill, I'll give you a $100 bill," then you would leave it!

You never know when you will need to use the *leave it!* cue. When I first moved back to North Carolina in 2009, I was taking my three dogs for a walk. I knew that Morgan had picked up something in her mouth, but honestly, I wasn't sure what it was. I cued "leave it," and to my disbelief, Morgan proceeded to spit an entire six-inch Subway® sandwich out of her mouth and then proudly looked at me. To this day, I am still amazed that Morgan listened to me because the sandwich was such a high value item to her. Training pays off. You never know what your dog might find, might get into, or what strangers may offer him. Teaching *leave it!* is a safety cue in addition to helping with impulse control and focus. It's a great tool to have when walking on leash.

How to Teach "Leave it!":

When using the cue *leave it!* you will need to treat with equal level treats or ask your dog to leave a lower level treat and reward with a higher level treat. A higher level treat for my dogs would be a hot-dog, and a lower level treat would be a piece of their dog food. Every dog will vary in preference just like humans. Some of us would enjoy chicken over steak, for example. The point is that you are asking your dog to leave the $50 and giving a $100.

Never release your dog to go get the treat or item you just told him to leave. Be consistent.

The *leave it!* cue is always cued first (unlike other taught behaviors and cues). The reason for this is your dog will know that if you don't want him to get or touch something, you always say "leave it!" But if you were to throw a ball or a treat and the dog didn't hear the "leave it!" cue, he is free to go for it!

Steps for teaching "leave it!":

1. Show your dog the treat. Cue "leave it!" Place the treat under your shoe. Your dog can dig at the shoe, stare at the shoe, but what you will be watching for is him looking up at you, looking away, or hopefully backing away. If the dog does any of these behaviors, click and treat. Repeat the game. You will not move on to the next step until he is consistently and quickly looking away, looking at you or backing up when you cue "leave it!"

Photo by Cheryl Kenyon
Michelle is cueing Boy to "leave it!"

2. This time, place a treat beside your shoe, but be ready to cover the treat quickly with your shoe if he goes for it. You will be watching for him to look up at you, look away, or

hopefully back away. When he does any of these actions, click and treat. Repeat the game. You will not move onto the next step until he is consistently and quickly looking away, looking at you or backing up when you cue "leave it!"

Photo by Cheryl Kenyon

Michelle is placing treat beside her shoe.

Photo by Cheryl Kenyon

Boy looked at Michelle's face, so Michelle clicked and rewarded.

3. Start dropping the treat from a higher level.

Photo by Cheryl Kenyon

Note: If you have a petite breed or a dog with less vigor, then using your hand rather than your shoe to cover up the treat is totally acceptable. I have included pictures below demonstrating using a fist/hand for the first process of teaching "leave it!" In the past five years I have started using my shoe because my hand had been "dug at" with paws way too many times.

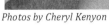
Photos by Cheryl Kenyon

Michelle is making a fist around the treat.

Photo by Cheryl Kenyon

Make a fist and push against ground. In this picture Boy looked away after hearing the "leave it!" cue, so Michelle clicked and rewarded him.

Photos by Cheryl Kenyon

The next step is to leave the treat uncovered.

On the remaining steps, you will not proceed until your dog is consistent and quick to respond. Again what you will be watching for is for him looking away, looking at you, or backing away.

4. Start by dropping several treats from one inch off the ground.

Photo by Cheryl Kenyon

5. Drop one treat from a higher distance.
6. Drop several treats from a higher distance.
7. Start by throwing one treat beside the dog. (Be sure you can cover it up if he goes for the treat)

Photo by Cheryl Kenyon

8. Throw one treat toward the dog.

9. Throw one treat beside the dog.
10. Throw several treats beside the dog.
11. Throw one treat toward the dog.
12. Throw several treats toward the dog.

Photo by Cheryl Kenyon

13. Place a treat on the dog's paw while working toward placing several.
14. Start generalizing your position. If you were sitting, stand now and start at the beginning steps.
15. Take this actively to new locations, but be sure to start at the beginning steps and work up.
16. Now start working on the cue *leave it!* Cue with neutral objects. (Remember, neutral objects have no emotional response from your dog such as a pencil.)
17. Now use the cue *leave it!* with more desired objects. After your dog is doing well in a formal session, you can cue "leave it!" with objects that you plant for him to find in the house or yard. Be sure to reward with equal or higher value. For example: when I ask my dog to leave the Loofa® stuffed dog. I will reward with his tennis ball and a game of fetch.
18. Start using *leave it!* with people that the dog knows. Allow your dog to go up to this person and cue "leave it!"

Good Things Come to Those Who Wait

Besides doing the training exercises written in this chapter, you can incorporate training that promotes impulse control into your everyday life as well. Having a pushy, demanding, or impatient dog is not good for the owner, but it also demonstrates the lack of impulse control on the dog's part.

What a pushy or impatient dog could look like

A pushy or impatient dog barks at you for supper, grabs at your pant leg to drag you to the door to go for a walk, or pushes his head under your hand to pet him.

How to work towards impulse control in everyday life

If you see that your dog wants to play ball, and he is jumping and you are in the mood to play ball cue a "sit," wait a few seconds, and then throw the ball. Be sure that you require him to "say please." In other words, cue a "sit" or cue a "down" before you throw the ball. Doing so will teach your dog to sit instead of using other forms of pushy behavior like jumping, barking, or pushing his head under your hand.

For example, when your dog is demanding something, ignore him because he is not using polite behavior. So if he pushes his hand under your hand, you can just nonchalantly move your hand away and continue to read your magazine or watch TV. A few moments later, you can call your dog over, ask for a "sit," and pet him.

When you get the leash for a walk and he is running all over the house, instead of chasing him, stand still holding the leash. When he comes over to you, ask for a "sit." If he sits and you start to clip on the leash, and he immediately stands before you even bend all the way down, simply stand back up. Wait for a sit and continue to repeat until he is sitting. This may take a while for the first few weeks, but it will work. You are using the Premack Principle (explained in more detail in chapter 7). The Premack Principle, simply stated, is that you get the behavior you want, then you give your dog what he wants, or in this case, a walk.

Incorporating these activities into your everyday life allows for multiple training opportunities to work on impulse control throughout the day. And, once you have accomplished—or at least made significant progress in teaching your dog impulse control—your chances for a successful leash walking experience multiply greatly!

CHAPTER 5

BIOFEEDBACK WITH LEASH WALKING

"We have not been informed that our bodies tend to do what they are told if we know how to tell them." – Elmer Green

I have been fascinated with biofeedback since I was first introduced to it four years ago; so fascinated, in fact, that I am dedicated to additional education so I can be a part of conducting research. One of the first questions that I am asked is, "What is biofeedback?"

The word biofeedback started being used in the 1960s when scientists were working with experimental tests to alter brain activity, blood pressure, and bodily functions that are not controlled voluntarily. At that time, scientists were looking forward to the day when biofeedback gave us major control over our own bodies. Some hoped that biofeedback would allow us to do away with drug treatments that often caused uncomfortable side effects. Research has proven that biofeedback helps in the treatment of many painful conditions and diseases.

Veterinarian and animal behaviorist, Dr. Karen Overall, explains biofeedback this way:

Heart rate, attentiveness and respiratory rate are all linked. If we can teach a human or a dog to take slower, deeper breaths, they relax, their heart rate decreases, and they can be more attentive to focusing on the task at hand. These responses are all coupled to changes in hormonal and other chemical signals that shift the brain's and body's reactivity from a system ready to act on a threat to one ready to focus on learning.[McDevitt, Leslie, Control Unleashed The Puppy Program 131]

Arizona Behavior Health Associates explains biofeedback as:

Like a pitcher learning to throw a ball across a home plate, the biofeedback trainee, in an attempt to improve a skill, monitors the performance. When a pitch is off the mark, the ballplayer adjusts the delivery so that he performs better the next time he tries. When the light flashes or the beeper beeps too often, the biofeedback trainee makes internal adjustments which alter the signals. The biofeedback therapist acts as a coach, standing at the sidelines setting goals and limits on what to expect and giving hints on how to improve performance.

Kjell Sheldon Nelson describes biofeedback as:

..a patient-guided treatment that teaches an individual to control muscle tension, pain, body temperature, brain waves, and other bodily functions and processes through relaxation, visualization, and other cognitive control techniques.

Neurotherapy, also known as "neurofeedback" and "EEG Biofeedback," is another form of biofeedback that helps a person learn how to modify brainwave activity to improve attention and control hyperactive behaviors.

With neurotherapy there are different noninvasive tools used to give the human feedback. Scientists first discovered neurofeedback using cats as their subjects, so I believe it is not too far of a stretch to use these techniques with dogs. During these studies, the cats, which had been given toxic chemicals known to cause seizures, were trained with specific brain frequencies, and the cats could then block the normal convulsive effects. This experiment was later found effective with monkeys and humans as well.

During neurotherapy the brain learns how to function efficiently in many ways. The two important ways are through operant conditioning and through classical conditioning. The basic principle of operant conditioning is that responses that are followed by pleasant or positive events are likely to be repeated and those followed by negative events occur with less frequency. When Barry Sterman wanted to teach cats to increase a particular brain wave (SMR), he structured the experimental situation so that when the rhythm increased, the cat would get a small taste of chicken broth and milk. This same procedure is used today..... to change the brainwaves. [Swingle, Paul, Biofeedback for the Brain 50]

Specifically, biofeedback gives a human feedback to help control heart rate and to help maintain a homeostatic state.

The brain can only be in one of two stages, either reactive or focused. If we can teach our dogs to breathe in a stressful or new situation, their reaction will be different. This is true as well for humans. When we get upset, we tend to hold our breath, and then things spiral out of control from there. But if we are involved in an upsetting situation and we continue to breathe, our reaction is completely different.

When I started hearing about biofeedback and neurotherapy, I immediately started thinking about the many possibilities with dogs, but, first things first, I decided to investigate biofeedback for myself. I wanted to know how it felt and how I personally would improve (or not improve). So I contacted the Soldier Wellness Center at Fort Bragg, North Carolina, to learn more about biofeedback, and in this chapter I am going to talk about my journey through this experience and how all these amazing techniques can be applied in dog training.

What is stress?
In my first session with the Wellness Center, we talked about stress, discussions which began with myself asking the question, "What is stress?"

The Online Merriam-Webster Dictionary offers the following two definitions:

A physical, chemical, or emotional factor that causes bodily or mental tension and may be a factor in disease causation

A state resulting from a stress; especially: one of bodily or mental tension resulting from factors that tend to alter an existent equilibrium

We talked about wellness for humans, so I next asked myself *what is wellness for dogs?* There are different elements to wellness including physical, emotional, intellectual, spiritual, social, and occupational (I still feel this definition and the various elements are applicable to dogs but in the sense of their daily activities.)

Stress is different for each person just as it is different for each dog. What situation I find stressful, you may find that you shrug your shoulders and not give the same situation another thought. Someone may find something as minor as chipping a nail to be extremely upsetting whereas someone else may lose their home and experience severe stress. Stress is based on the perception of each individual person and thus will likewise be based on each individual dog's perspective. Just as for humans, *whether stress is real or imagined, the body reacts.*

What is the dog's perception of stress?
My friend Kristen and I were visiting Wilmington, NC, recently when we were about to cross a bridge that had struck anxiety in me before. I told Kristen to prepare herself to see me work on some target training to control my emotional reaction to crossing that bridge and to trust that I would be a lot more obvious and loud about it if she weren't in my car. She started laughing. The kind of bridge we were crossing stresses me out even right now as I am typing about it. My heart rate has changed, and I am pretty sure that my hands are slightly moist from perspiration. This bridge has a metal surface, and when the tires of the car go over the bridge, it feels as though the metal is pulling my car every which way, and the sound that it makes doesn't help. When I go over the bridge, I usually target my breath with loud yoga Hatha breathing. I know I sound ridiculous as I describe this event and my efforts to control my stress, but if it gets me across the bridge without a panic attack, that's just good for everyone involved.

If you asked my friend that actually lives in Wilmington what her reaction is when she crosses that bridge, she probably would shrug her shoulders and not think twice because she grew up in the area and probably goes over the bridge often.

Just like humans, every dog will react differently to different stimuli. What matters as the handler is that you recognize what the stressor is for your dog from your dog's point of view.

Often times, we mean well when we train and attempt to help our dog "get over" his stress, but many times we can make problems worse. A good example of this would be if a dog seems uncomfortable around people, the pet owner responds by having every person hand treats to the dog. In our minds, we reason that if people are giving treats, then the dog associates the good thing with those people. The problem, in most cases, is that the dog doesn't change his perspective of the stressor. In fact, his stress level has increased because now he is forced to interact with the very people that were stressing him in the first place.

This is like asking me to pet a rattle snake and then having the rattle snake "hand" me a $50 bill. I don't want to pet a rattle snake ever, not even for a $50 bill, and now they are coming in close proximity.

So, if a dog's stressor is people, then play a game such as having him look at the person, delivering the treat every time he looks. I would be able to handle looking at a rattlesnake from a distance and being rewarded with a $50 bill by my best friend; which is how your dog may perceive you. Forcing me to take a $50 bill out of the mouth of the snake is a very stressful thought, just as taking treats out of a human's hand could be to a dog. It becomes a simple matter of seeing situations from your dog's point of view and reacting accordingly.

Good Stress versus Bad Stress

Good stress may occur in the form of a deadline that needs to be met, and so you are focused, pumped, and fired up to go until the project is complete. With good stress, we take charge. Bad stress, on the other hand, might be a co-worker that is causing you so much anxiety you have a stomach ache. With bad stress we need to learn coping skills, serenity, and the ability to sometimes say "no."

Likewise, there are good stressors for your dog. An example of good

> *There are good stressors and bad stressors. Good stress involves the dog feeling like he can take charge. With bad stress we need to teach our dog coping skills and serenity, and maybe sometimes allow him to just walk away. –Michelle Huntting*

stress would be in clicker training when we mark a behavior and continue to mark the same behavior. Soon a handler will raise a criterion by delaying the click to see what the dog will do. It's during this process that the dog may experience some stress, but in the process will show several different behaviors that the trainer can then choose from and click the exact desired behavior.

The Handler's Role: Manager

As a handler, you are the one that understands and knows your dog. Even if I were to come in and work with your dog, yes, I would be able to read his body language, but I will not know him as you do. Even if the most skilled canine body language reader came to work with Ellie, my Bloodhound, he or she may not notice that right before she "loses it" her forehead will slightly wrinkle up. I realized early on in my relationship with Ellie that when I saw that slight wrinkle, I needed to quickly adjust how the environment looked to her. Handlers should be able to clue in on their dog's cues. Similarly, within a human partnership, you know things about that person that no one else knows, and you always learn when to approach that partner about a subject and when not to. It's all about becoming well aware of each other's needs and learning what the other can handle. If you notice that your dog is uncomfortable, and you believe it is the environment that is making him uncomfortable, you may need to eliminate that environment if it is possible to do so. For example, if he is showing stress in a dog park, the solution may be as simple as not taking him to the dog park again. Maybe it is a necessary environment, such as the vet's office, and you do need to take your dog there. While you are there, you notice that your dog is beginning to become uncomfortable. Recognizing his cues, you may need to adjust the environment by beginning some body work or cueing him to breathe. You are his manager. Yes, you've given him the tools to learn how to use his body, and the more you practice and work with him, the more he will understand how to use his body on his own, but overall, you are his manager of stress.

Trigger Stacking

We've all been there. As you are driving to work, someone cuts you off. You get to the office, and someone says something that is really irritating. Your client calls and rips on you, and your order that was supposed to be there "just in time" for an event comes in wrong. You handle all of these stressors successfully, making sure you are breathing, and calming your client down so you can create a solution. You finally make it home at the end of a long, stressful day that you have brilliantly managed, and as soon as you walk in the door, your spouse scolds you about forgetting to pick up the milk for the kids, who at this point are screaming, and the dog just peed on your foot. You lose it. You yell at your spouse and leave the room to let off some steam.

This scenario is what we call trigger stacking. If stressors are addressed individually, they can be successfully resolved, but when one thing continues to happen after another, you can no longer handle it and you "lose it." In the dog world, this reaction would be called *going over the threshold.*

This is what happens to dogs: I have heard clients say, "He's never like that," and they are probably right. The dog's behavior wasn't a true reflection of him, but with all the triggers stacked, he reacted. The environment can be a contributing factor. For example, you take your dog out for a walk, and a yappy dog lunges as it walks by, but you both successfully get through this moment. Then, a motorcycle revs as you walk by a bit later. You make it to the baseball diamond to watch your niece play her softball game and it's a hot summer day.

All of the kids now are starting to bombard your cute dog to pet him, and, lo and behold, though it is completely out of his nature, he growls. This reaction more than likely was caused from "trigger stacking."

A trigger can be anything that your dog finds stressful. It could be a dog looking at him the wrong way or a child screaming loudly or the heat of the day. Just like humans, every dog will be different. It's important to observe your dog to see what his triggers (or stressors) are. Remember the signs of stress (in chapter 3) from his body language, and realize that these signs can be very subtle.

Just as it is very uncommon for you to yell at your spouse and leave the room, so it is also uncommon for your dog to growl. It's important to be aware of contributing factors as you are out and about with your dog on leash. Know his limits and pay attention to what's going on around you and how your dog is behaving. Be your dog's advocate and help him manage his stress.

Coherence and Homeostatic State

Coherence is being aware of the body in order to control heart function. –Michelle Huntting

All of the following systems or components come together affecting the level of coherence: physical (the body), emotional (perception), and the mind (thoughts). If the body is in pain, the emotions run high; or if the mind is racing, then there will not be a balanced breathing rhythm, and thus the heart will not be coherent with the other systems.

On my first day of biofeedback session, I was honestly a little scared. I had read so much about this subject and knew that it was noninvasive, but there was still the element of the unknown. I sat in a massage chair for a while, and then my coach came back into the room to start working on biofeedback. She placed an instrument that measured my heart rate on my ear lobe.

My first day of biofeedback. Can you tell I am a little uneasy from my body language? You can see in the picture I have the monitor attached to my ear lobe.

Photo by biofeedback coach

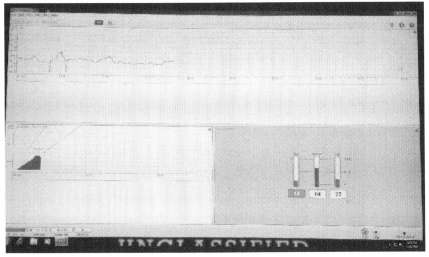

Photo by author

This chart is an example of my baseline breathing. If you look at the top chart, the lines are jagged and erratic. The bottom right shows that I am functioning at 64 percent coherence, which means that something (physical, mental, or emotional) is "off," not allowing for 100 percent coherence.

As I was in the biofeedback chair hooked up to my ear piece, I listened to a coach as we started our training session. The screen that was in front of me had these large upside down "u" shapes that looked like rounded mountain tops. There was a curser that moved slowly up and down the rounded mountain tops. The curser was a visual aid to help me target the rhythm of my breathing. The curser moved up as I was breathing in and down as I let out my breath. This was not easy. At this point my heart rate was peaking with a lot of jagged lines. I finally started focusing (targeting) on my breathing. I realized when the exercise was over that I had stopped thinking about the million things that I had to do, the million things I forgot to do, and what I was making for supper. I thought about my breath. I made myself breathe in and breathe out. My biofeedback coach showed me the difference on my chart. Now my lines showed the beautiful upside down "u" shaped mountains that this time reflected my rate of over 80 percent coherence, much improved from my base line of 64 percent.

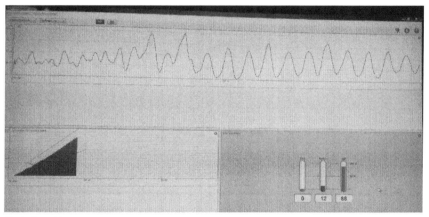

Photo by author

With the help of a breathing coach, I was able to have a consistent rhythm to my breathing and make a more steady round response on the chart and also become 88 percent coherent.

As I was going through this exercise, I became very aware of how lack of sleep was affecting my breathing, revealing to me the physical aspect of biofeedback. In order for my body to be functioning at coherence, I needed more sleep.

Also I became aware of the lack of thought I put into my breathing. I do yoga and at least one meditation at the end of the day, so at these times, I focus on my breath. But I realized, as I am going about the business of my daily life, I don't give my breathing pattern much thought. On my way home from my session, I thought to myself, *what if I did?* What if I started focusing on my breathing throughout the day? Would I see a difference? Would I feel calm? More focused? Be more productive?

Body as a Whole

It's important to look at the body in the entirety- body, mind, and soul. My body is not going to function at its full capacity if I do not eat well or sleep right. If I allow something to trouble my mind, then my mind will become caught up in another issue instead of focusing on tasks at hand. If my spirit is not in tune with my "gut" feelings, then I am going against what is right for me. All of these phenomena, integrate, and must align for my body to function in the state of homeostasis.

The Dog's Body

Appropriate Diet. I believe what I have described to be the same for dogs as well. It starts with a great diet. (Please see chapter 16 for an article by Kim Matsko, a nutrition specialist.) It's important that dogs get a proper species-appropriate diet, including food and treats without high fructose corn syrup, fillers, and artificial additives.

Appropriate Rest. Appropriate, adequate rest is essential for all beings, and so it is for dogs. I don't know what your home life looks like, but if you come for a visit at my house, even for an hour, you will see how busy twin three-year olds can be. In this type of high-activity environment (not to mention loud and draining!), my dogs have a room of their own where they can slip away from it all. Rest isn't just sleep; it's also a breather away from the hubbub of activity and potential stressors. Please be aware that just as you need a moment to yourself to get recharged, so do dogs.

Appropriate Exercise. The amount of exercise needed by each dog will be based on the age and the breed. Regardless, it is important that he gets physical exercise outside of the home whether it's going for a walk around the neighborhood or park, or playing ball in the backyard. Remember that in addition to physical exercise, he also needs mental exercise. Many games can be found on the Internet that are fun to play with your dog. Trick training is enjoyable, along with scent detection type games, and some puzzle games that can be purchased (Nina Ottosson www.nina-ottosson.com).

A Dog's Mind (Emotions)

The mind of a dog, oh how we long to understand it and would love to "get inside." What we've learned about a dog's mind has come from observation. What I've observed many times when conducting in-home sessions with dogs is stimulation overload. Many owners leave the TV or radio on thinking that this will help their dog relax, but, from their behavior, I am not observing relaxation in any way whatsoever. There are CDs that have been created that are clinically proven to help dogs relax, so those would be my recommendation if you feel that some sort of sound in the background would be beneficial. It would be better to leave on soothing nature sounds (like the ocean waves) versus the television or radio. It is my observation that dogs are exposed to constant stimuli. Really, as humans our lives are very loud. Dogs don't need or want the same kind of stimulation that we do.

A Dog's Soul

Their spirit is an element to their state of homeostatis. Perhaps the element of spirit in a dog's life is their life purpose. I have observed from watching different competitive dog sports that it seems, at times, the human would like to be involved with the sport or activity more than the dog. It's important that as owners we observe and see what they truly find enjoyable and help them pursue that purpose whether it's therapy, service, search and rescue, scent detection, or just enjoying being a stay-at-home dog.

Breathe, Just Breathe

In stressful situations I learned to focus on my breath. If I can, I take a break, walk with breathing, and step away from the situation for a few minutes. Dogs can learn to do so too. We can remove them momentarily from a situation to help them maintain focus. We can also teach them how to breathe.

How can the breathing techniques apply to dogs? Well, for me, target breathing helped me forget about my stress. Because of an overwhelming amount of mental stress, focusing on my breathing was, well, let's just say, it needed much improvement. Once I started targeting, I forgot about everything else. It was an "aha" moment. My mind went quiet. Wow, that is rare. I could actually hear myself think and feel a sense of peace come over me. I liked this feeling. I would like to revisit that feeling. Likewise, dogs enjoy peace. They also enjoy being relaxed. Those two things, I believe, are self-reinforcing, just like endorphins after a run. You and your dog want to revisit this "place."

We can teach our dogs to breathe on cue. To do so, you will need treats and a clicker. Hold a treat directly in front of your dog's nose and watch for his nostrils to flair out. When you see them flair out (which shows a breath), you will click and give him the treat. Repeat this exercise. Once you've completed several sessions of this exercise, then you can add a cue. The idea for this technique is credited to Dr. Overall.

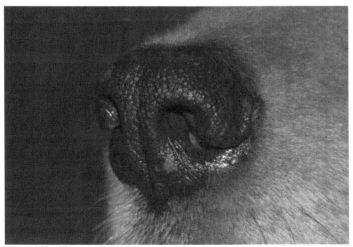

Photo by Cheryl Kenyon

Boy's Nose

Photo by Cheryl Kenyon

Look at the sides of boy's nose as they are flaring out.

To visit a demo video of me training Boy's nose flare, visit, www.michellehuntting.com/demo.html

What if my dog tries to bite the treat? If this happens, I simply turn my hand in toward me so he is not able to get it. There is an example picture of this on page 206. Usually my dogs will respond with re-sitting for me. If your dog doesn't reposition in a sit, then cue a "sit" and begin the exercise all over again.

Trouble shooting: If your dog has a tendency to touch your hand when you are holding the treat or has a frequent tendency to go for the treat, you can use something other than a treat such as an essential oil or an empty can of dog food instead of the treat and watch his nostrils flare as he breathes in the beautiful scent.

Week Two
I began my second visit to the Army Wellness Center sitting in the zero gravity chair for 20 minutes, surrounded by the relaxing environment, and then we started with the biofeedback training.

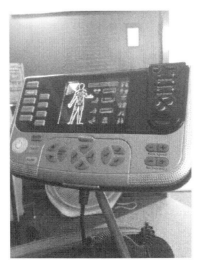

Photo taken by author

My baseline showed an improved score from last week, which didn't surprise me. The previous week I had just finished editing and submitting my first book *Gotta Go! Successfully Potty Train Your Dog,* and I know that I was completely exhausted. I had learned a great deal from the previous session. Today, however, I noticed how difficult it was for me to even focus on my breath. I didn't want to. It took everything in my body, mind, and willpower to do it. Instead I wanted to focus on what needed to be done that day how I couldn't wait until my session was over because I was going shopping, which hadn't happened in a while, wondering about my phone that kept vibrating, and thinking about this book all at once. It took great energy to just shove all of that to the side and breathe in and out, focusing on my breath just for the base line. The training allowed me to reach 100 percent, which was shocking to me because the amount of stress I was experiencing was overwhelming, but I was able to train my body to maintain a coherent state.

Do I look any more relaxed in my body language? This is week two with biofeedback, and I am sitting in a zero gravity chair before we start working on the breathing techniques.

After we finished the baseline, I started talking to my coach about biofeedback. Why is it so difficult to be in homeostatic state? I am still fascinated with the question of why this doesn't come naturally to us. Even when children get upset, they hold their breath, scream, cry, and their entire energy elevates from there. And as a mommy of toddler twin boys, I am truly speaking from numerous observational hours. At times, I have to speak in a softer tone and use my own deep breathing to help encourage them to begin breathing again.

When we are highly stressed we hold our breath or our breathing becomes shallow. When someone is yelling at us on the phone, for example, if we can visualize and make sure that the air touches the bottom of the lungs before the air leaves, this will ease the stressful situation and enable your mind to be clear to help talk the person down into a calmer state.

Why is it so difficult to be in a relaxed state? It doesn't come naturally at all. Even my coach said that it is a *learned state*. I see this being true for dogs as well. They don't naturally know how to make themselves calm down, and neither do we.

The body strives to stay in a homeostatic state. If the heart rate increases, the body temperature increases, trying to maintain the body in a homeostasic state.

How can biofeedback apply to dog training? I am assuming that dogs' bodies are similar, in that, based upon my observation, they don't automatically know how to relax. Rather, my experience tells me that relaxation can only happen with the help and good judgment of the handler. The handler is required to watch the dog's body for cues of distress, the beginning of stress, and to help adjust the environment, and to provide that "break" away from the stressful environment or to even cue a breath to remind the dog to breathe.

I see the same signals of stress from dogs that humans experience-holding their breath, dilated pupils, short heavy breaths, stiffness, sweat from the paws. I have seen them shut down to the point where they physically appear to not be present, not to be able to hear or react to the sound of their handler's voice, similar to a human in severe stress. If all these things are so similar, then why wouldn't biofeedback training work the same for a dog? The key is figuring out the elements of training to teach the biofeedback methods to maintain a coherent state.

Week Three

This week we focused on visualization. Before we started, I was excited, and I shared that excitement with my biofeedback coach. I love doing visualization. She asked if I had done this before? I told her that I had done a lot of meditation with yoga, and I really enjoy it. I went on to tell her about my labor experience with my twins.

When I was 29 weeks pregnant, my water broke, and the doctors decided that it was best to continue my labor for as long as they could. I ended up being in labor for five days, and one of the ways I made it through the unbearable pain was using visualization. In my mind, I went to a beautiful forest. This forest looked like the Carolina forests. The sun was positioned at the tops of the trees shining warmly on my face. When the pain was extremely bad, though, I started using targeting. I concentrated on my breath, not the pain. I made sure that I breathed in, held it, and let it go only to repeat it again.

My description of this experience amazed my biofeedback coach. I think I'm still a little amazed myself because I had never really been taught this strategy for managing pain. We then started going through the visualization techniques for our session together. This week I scored the best that I had ever scored with biofeedback. She pointed out that my breath was deeper.

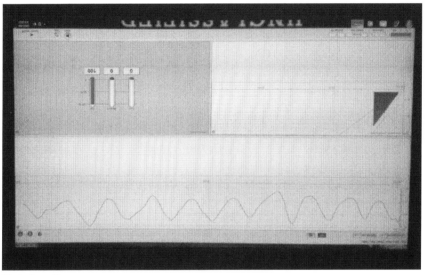

Photo by author

This chart reflects how relaxed I was. Out of all the weeks of biofeedback, this was the best one for me, demonstrating that visualization is one of the better techniques for me to use when stressed.

My thought when I left the Wellness Center was *how can visualization apply when working with dogs to help them relieve stress?* I think that I found the answer in the next few weeks of considering this question.

Carefully selected, appropriate music will help them go to a "happy place." A few months ago, I interviewed Lisa Spector on my radio show *Dog Talk*. Lisa created clinically proven CDs for dogs called-*Through a Dog's Ear.* After our interview together, I started incorporating the CD with my training. At the time, I was training a dog with severe separation anxiety. Every single day the owners were coming home to a very wet dog from his saliva. Obviously, there are many more details concerning this particular case, but one of the tools that we used with him was *Through a Dog's Ear*. The first week, they came home to a dry dog three days out of five. Typically, he was wet five days out of five, even with the medication he was taking.

I have been amazed by the results that I've seen from this CD series. Recently, a portable device came out that can be played when you take your dog out for a walk, to the vet, or anywhere. I believe that this is a great tool to help a dog go to their "happy place."

For additional information visit, www.throughadogsear.com.

Week Four
This day was the most difficult of all the weeks of training to able to focus on my breathing in order to maintain the coherent state. As I have mentioned before, at the beginning of each session, the coach takes a baseline of your breathing. I was able to maintain 100 percent with just my baseline, but it took so much effort on my part. I had so much on my mind about work, deadlines, my children, and the list goes on. I didn't want to focus on my breath. Every time I did, all those other things kept popping up, but I had to make myself target on my breath.

I can imagine that dogs (even though they don't have the to-do list) have, at times, an overwhelming number of emotions tied to something, and it may take a *great* effort for them to focus. We can see from observation their efforts to focus some times. Obviously, we don't know what they are thinking, but we can watch their body language and see that they are overly alert in an environment which tells me they are concerned about something and often times are severely stressed. In those times, it is extremely difficult for them to focus, and the handler needs to make the call whether it's just best to go on a short walk or send them to bed (literally).

As for myself and my own biofeedback training on this day, my body, mind, and emotions had hit their limit and I was just done (a bit of trigger stacking here). So, I officially put myself in a time-out.

I also believe that this can happen to a dog when guests that they are not used to are in the home, or if the guests are loud. The dog may need a timeout. There may be children involved who have good intentions as they continue to try to pet your dog, but your dog was "just done" hours before. It is important to be aware of your dog's state and remove your dog into a safe environment (even a kennel).

In one of my group classes that I teach outdoors, I require students to bring along a kennel for this very reason. I remember one specific class where the dog was overly alert to the environment, constantly looking all around, ears moving around, and never relaxed. I recommended to the owner that she put him in her wire crate. The owner kept refusing, even questioning how much good that would do. Finally, she gave in to my suggestions, and as soon as the dog got into the kennel, even with the door open, we could all see the dog sigh and relax within seconds. I believe the dog was concerned that other dogs and humans in the park were going to come up to him, and the kennel served as a relief because he was "safe."

It's important to pay attention to your dog's body language and, when necessary, remove him from the environment by calling a "time-out."

Using Scent for Relaxation

Scent is a very powerful tool. I know for myself, smelling just one scent can send a million memories through my mind within seconds. Breathing in lavender essential oil helps me begin to instantly relax. Scent can change our moods very quickly. You can use scent to help your dog to relax and focus. I have included two great companies in this chapter that have products that I have used myself and that I feel comfortable in promoting their high quality products.

Young Living®

Many essential oils that are available on the market are synthetic and full of chemicals. There are very few essential oils that are pure enough to be called medical grade or even safe to use on pets. Young Living® has become my first choice for essential oils. The company organically grows their own crops of high quality species and processes the plants to maintain the highest grade medicinal oils possible.

Peace & Calming is a blend of Blue Tansy, Patchouli, tangerine, orange, and Ylang Ylang. This blend has been used for anxiety, stress, hyperactivity, car sickness, when boarding and crating for travel, and overall, to aid where calming is needed. This oil can also be diffused into the air.

Lavender can be used in an air diffuser and also directly applied. According to holistic veterinarian Melissa Shelton, 1 drop of Lavender can be diluted in 2 drops of Young Living's® V-6 and applied once or twice a day for each 20 pounds of body weight.

Some handlers apply the oils on themselves, and the dog is able to breathe in the oil scent and receive the benefits this way as well.

To order Young Living® products visit, www.youngliving.com.

Bach's Flower Rescue Remedy®

Dr. Edward Bach discovered the original remedies. The Rescue Remedy® is a blend of 5 different flowers (Star of Bethlehem, Cherry Plum, Rock Rose, Clematis, and Impatiens). These fragrances promote relaxation during a stressful situation and help with focus. To find more information on the Rescue Remedy®, or to order visit, www.bachflower.com.

Awww... Relaxed: Body Training

The feeling of being relaxed in and of itself is reinforcing. Additional strategies to promote relaxation are TTouch® and massage.

TTouch® was developed by Linda Tellington-Jones. This approach is designed for companion animals, exotic animals, horses, and humans. This method uses specific points on animals or humans in a circular motion. The procedure can help enhance the quality of life, often times aiding in behavioral challenges and, at the same time, promote relaxation. You can find books, DVDs, and training seminars at www.ttouch.com.

In addition, in Chapter 16 you can view an entire article written by Kristen McCartney, an animal massage therapist, on all the benefits of massage for dogs. I know we automatically think of a luxurious spa treatment, but massage can produce many positive effects for your dog.

As I said, experiencing the feeling of relaxation in and of itself is reinforcing, and the more your dog can experience the feeling, the easier it will be for him to revisit that feeling. I know this to be true from dogs that I have worked with but also from my own biofeedback experience. Once I learned the breathing techniques and knew what it felt like, I was quickly able to return my body to that state even in stressful situations.

Overall
All of these tools can be applied and used for your dog to work toward relaxation and focus while out on a walk. Being out on a walk with your dog is so much more than having him just strolling at your left side; it's being relaxed and focused in a rich and sometimes stressful environment. Teaching him the relaxation skills ahead of time that can then be "taken on the road" and quickly pulled as resources, whether he chooses to do it on his own or you cue him, can lead to a pleasurable and positive experience. In my experience, and I hope yours, biofeedback is another great tool for leash walking.

CHAPTER 6

TARGET FOR RELAXATION

I mentioned that I targeted my breath as part of stress management. I find that many parts to stress management involve targeting. In August I had a book signing in Virginia for my first book. It was a long drive to do by myself, but I was fine. However, on the way home it was storming. I was in a rental car so I wasn't as comfortable as I normally would be in my own vehicle. The rain was coming down so strong that I could hardly see much of the time. My strategy during those hours driving home on the interstate was to watch the bumper of the red car in front of me. As long as I could see that car, I felt a sense of peace and assurity that I'd be okay. I was able to target on something to forget about my stressor (or at least ease my stressor).

On another occasion when I was at a large training conference, one of the well-known trainers was sharing a story with us about her therapy dog. They were visiting in a nursing home when she noticed that her dog felt uncomfortable, so she started observing more closely. She noticed while they were walking down the hallway that every time they passed an open door, her dog was uncomfortable, so she began to use her hand as a target when they would come across an open door. Her dog began to relax.

Targeting can involve any object, even a place, as long as you focus on something specific. I started doing weight resistance training a few weeks ago. I have never tried this kind of training before, so all of it was very new. But I thought I would give it a try since the television commercial guaranteed that I would look amazing at the end of a month. There was one particular exercise that I thought I wouldn't be able to do. I had to start in a squat position while I was holding a bar, and I had to stand straight up while keeping my back straight the entire time. I was really psyching myself out, arching my back and thinking I couldn't do it. So I started targeting a specific spot on the wall, and my entire form changed. Targeting with my eyes helped me focus on something other than the stress caused from the thought of *I can't do this.*

Targeting is essential for both dogs and people to learn to relax in stressful situations. The target can be touching something, focusing on breathing, looking at something, or going to a specific place with an end destination targeted.

Target with Eyes

I have included many target exercises you can perform with the eyes to include *w-a-t-c-h* and *check-ins* on page 203. I have also included marking a *look* in the *let's go* exercise.

Exercise: The distracted dog is a great exercise for learning how to target with the eyes. This exercise can be found on page 40.

As you work on this exercise, you will be able to practice longer. Your dog may end up doing what Boy does. He will try to follow me, maintaining eye contact the entire time. So I tell him to "go sniff," and he will quickly put his nose down, still looking at me, hoping for a click and treat. Even though that antic is very cute, it's cheating, and I make sure I say Boy's name first and then watch for him to look back at me.

Target Hand

Hand targeting is a great tool because you won't forget to leave this tool at home as you will be able to use this exercise to modify any stressful situation, to gain focus on the leash when there are a lot of distractions, and so much more. In one of my group courses, we will use hand targeting on turns because that tends to be where dogs lose focus.

Exercise:

(Step 1) You can start with a repetition of eight, so count out eight treats and hold them in your non-dominant hand. Now, sitting down with your dog, place both hands behind your back. Present your dominant hand flat to your dog. If he doesn't touch and you've waited three seconds, return your hand back behind your back and quickly present again. Repeat this process until he touches. As soon as he touches, say the word "touch," praise, and deliver one treat. Repeat until all eight repetitions are finished.

You will know that your dog understands and is ready to move on with the next step when you present your hand and he quickly touches it. When this happens consistently every time, you can then move on to the next step.

(Step 2) Now do the same exercise only this time use the opposite hand for touch until he is consistent.

(Step 3) For the next step, we will start adding movement, so this time instead of putting your hand directly in front of you move it slightly to the right doing three repetitions, and then move the same hand to the left doing three repetitions. Once your dog is consistently touching your hand with slight movement, you can also move your hand below and above his head.

Photo by Bryan Huntting

The principles and steps of teaching hand targeting and object targeting are the exact same. Michelle is teaching Boy to go from side to side (step 3) with a target stick which in this case is a plastic spoon.

Photo by Bryan Huntting

(Step 4) Now it's time to stand up and walk two or three steps in front of your dog, and on your heel side, present your hand in the position that cues a touch, and say "touch." As soon as he puts his wet nose into your hand, praise and treat. Continue moving two to three steps at a time.

Photo by Bryan Huntting

Again the principles of teaching your dog to target a hand or a stick are the same. Michelle is taking a few steps at a time, presenting the target on her left side (Step 4). This helps reinforce the position of heel, with his head up, as well as maintaining his focus.

(Step 5) You will gradually increase the number of steps that you take, and you can also be creative with what you do. Touch is used for many different things, including tricks. For the sake of this book, however, we are using touch for focus on the leash as well as a stress reducer.

Note: Often times we have hand signals for cues. One of the most common cues to use a hand signal is "stay." I will use my hand flat out with the palm of my hand facing my dog, so it's important when you are teaching "touch" that your non-verbal cue, which is presenting your hand, looks different than any other cue.

Also, be specific in what kind of touch you reward. In other words, make sure that your dog's mouth is closed. We want to be specific with this as we don't want any teeth to even accidentally touch your skin.

Target Stick

The target stick is fantastic, and I use it as a demonstration in this book as well. I enjoy using something other than my hand probably because I am so tall, but with a target stick I don't have to bend at all. This tool is crucial for the petite breeds as the owner will more than likely not be able to use the hand as a target while on walks though he may for many other training activities. If you have a petite breed you can use a wooden dowel and put a soft ping pong ball on the end. On the other hand, if you have a giant breed, you can use something that is short. I bought a package of plastic spoons that included a very short spoon (maybe four inches) that would work well with giant breeds. I use many kitchen items including a spoon or rubber scraper. You can even purchase fancy target sticks. Whatever you want to use is fine as the principles to train are the same.

Target Stick Exercise: You will do the same steps involved with teaching how to target with the hand, but use a target stick in its place.

Remember to be specific in what you reward. Is it okay for them to touch up high on the stick? Personally, I want them to touch the wider area at the bottom, but that decision is up to each handler.

Target Left Side

I have used the target stick to help a client that was showing his dogs for confirmation. His dog was continually looking at the ground, sniffing, and this behavior wasn't working in the AKC show ring. The method to keep the dog's head up he had learned from a trainer was very interesting, but it was not working. Therefore, we used a target stick so the dog was not only getting reinforced for heeling but also for holding his head up from the ground. If you are a hound lover like me, or maybe just have a dog that loves to sniff, you can use this tool to reinforce holding the head up from the ground. Remember, to be specific in what you are reinforcing by making sure you work your dog on the heel side.

Heel: Using target in the heel exercise, I think, is a great way to encourage dogs to get a feel for the exact position and to maintain focus in a hands-off approach. As I have said, many times the turns seem to be more difficult for the dog, so if you are finding that you lose your dog's focus on almost every turn, you can present your hand a couple steps before the turn and continue presenting during the turn.

When I use a target (hand or object) during the heel, I will present my hand and say "touch" every so many steps and reward. You don't want to wait too long before rewarding.

Targeting a Specific Place
Sometimes using a *go to* cue can keep the dog's focus on something other than what's going on in the environment. A good example of this would be *go to mat.* For the sake of this leash walking book, I have not included exercises to teach a *go to mat* cue, but wanted to mention this concept as a stress releaser for dogs. Humans do a similar activity when running a race; we focus on the finish line which allows us to push through pain and the thoughts of quitting.

This *go to* cue can be anything. For example, let's say you were at the park, and something very stressful just happened for your dog. You take one look at him say, "Let's go for a ride." In that moment he targets getting to the car, allowing him to remove himself from the stressful environment. He was able to handle himself because he focused on getting to a specific place. The *go to* cue can be used with any place that you know your dog will enjoy.

Targeting for relaxation is yet another tool that will help set your dog up for success as you work toward effective leash walking.

CHAPTER 7

REINFORCEMENT

The reinforcements placed in a building cause the structure to be stronger. Without reinforcement, the building could not withstand sustained high winds. Reinforcement applied in exercise, such as lifting weights, causes our muscles to become stronger. Reinforcement is equally as important when applied in the training program.

Reinforcement is *the act of strengthening or encouraging something; a thing that strengthens or encourages something*
Online Merriams-Webster

What can be used as a reinforcement? Anything that your dog sees as desirable. Reinforcement, for you too, is something that you see as desirable. As humans, we all work for money. Money is a huge motivator, and we will do some great things for the sake of it. Money to a dog smells interesting, but I doubt that you could get more than three sits for a hundred dollar bill.

Aside from money, motivators can come in many different forms for humans. The environment and temperature can also be appealing reinforcements for us, depending on the time of year. Because they make us feel good, we gravitate toward the fan or fireplace.

When I am training a dog, I will use many reinforcers aside from food such as allowing him to chase a blowing leaf along the road or smell the "pee mail" (a tree or post where another male dog has marked) on the tree or a game of tug.

Reinforcement is always changing. I find this to be true, especially when training in the outdoors. One minute my dog desires a cooked hot-dog, and the next minute he wants to sniff the latest "pee mail" on the mail box post. Competing for attention when training in such a rich environment to a dog is something that can be viewed as a struggle, or you can look at it as an opportunity to be observant and to change your reinforcement to what your dog desires in that moment.

For example, your dog is pulling you because there is a specific patch of grass he would like to go sniff. We can either see that patch of grass as frustrating, or we can see it as an opportunity. Now is the time to think, *"Aha, puppy dog, you really want to go sniff those blades of grass, a beautiful opportunity. But, first, puppy, we must get there on a loose leash."* You will then use the *let's go* method, backing up every time he pulls until you can get a loose leash dangling down to those blades of grass.

Reinforcement is always chosen by the learner. I just mentioned a moment ago that I really doubt that you could get your dog to do more than three sits by rewarding with a hundred dollar bill. You might think, *"What's wrong with you?? I would do 20 sits for a hundred bucks!!"* But that is the difference between what humans view as desirable reinforcement and what a dog sees as desirable reinforcement. Whoever you are teaching or training is the one that gets to choose what's worth his time.

Timing matters. When you deliver treats or any other reinforcement, the timing is important. Imagine these two scenarios:

Show Treat → Call "come" → Dog comes → Deliver treat

Call "come"→ Dog comes → Deliver treat

Do you see the difference? It's important that you get the behavior 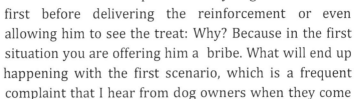 first before delivering the reinforcement or even allowing him to see the treat: Why? Because in the first situation you are offering him a bribe. What will end up happening with the first scenario, which is a frequent complaint that I hear from dog owners when they come the first night of class, is, "My dog will only lie down for a treat." Or another classic one is that the dog only comes when he hears the owner shaking the bag of treats. This is not good training nor will it give you the strong desired behaviors that I know you want. If you train using the treat first before the cue or behavior, you will always be stuck doing so. With good training skills, a handler will wait for the desired behavior and then deliver the treat.

Don't be stingy.
The number of treats (or length of time reinforcement is given) matters. In other words, if I have been working toward a specific behavior in a training session, and my dog finally performs that behavior, I will deliver a jackpot. A jackpot is several treats delivered one at a time, one right after the other. Just as for a person winning a jackpot of money on a slot machine, the method is a key to strengthening the dog's behavior for the next time. The big win keeps the human playing the slot machine because of the hope of a big pay off just as the dog will continue to work toward his big pay off in the form of a jackpot of treats.

On the other hand, this doesn't mean that you should deliver three treats at once every time you are reinforcing a behavior. Your dog will get fat this way. However, for the moments that you see the behaviors that are fantastic because they looked exactly how you wanted them to look, or your dog has been working hard in a session and he finally achieves the desired behavior, it's time to give a jackpot.

Remember though, a jackpot doesn't always have to come in the form of food. I was hired by a family to get their dog to *kennel up*, meaning the Lab had some issues with going into the kennel. I worked her for a while, and finally she went all the way into the kennel. I released the dog out of her kennel, and we played a three-minute game of tag and tug in the backyard. When we went to start our next training session for kennel up, she ran right back in and got another three-minute game around the yard, and then I ended the training session. Being skilled in reinforcement is a huge part of a successful training program.

Why aren't we generous?
We love our dogs. I know because most dogs that I train for have numerous toys and sometimes have a better prepared meal than I ever have time for. It amazes me that the same pet owner that purchased a Posturepedic® bed designed especially for dogs can be so stingy with the dog's reinforcements. The same people that work hard so their dog can live a comfortable life are often stingy with the treats and are uncomfortable using treats in training.

I really think that this notion stems from the idea of old training methods, and the misconception that food makes a dog a beggar. Giving dogs treats doesn't make them beggars anymore than paying you on the 1st and 15th of the month makes you a beggar. You worked, so you got paid. Treats are the same thing to a dog. As long as treats are used in the correct order and manner as previously described, then your dog is simply getting paid for doing his "job."

Get the behavior you want➔ Deliver the treat

How to view your treats

As you are working toward desired behavior (like eye contact, specific positions on leash), you will want to reinforce that behavior with food, praise, etc. Begin to view your treats, praise, or other reinforcers as money. Each time you deliver a treat, there is a coin going into your piggy bank of behavior. Before you know it, you have a pretty strong "bank of behavior" account.

What it will become

Obviously, as you work through the training process, and behaviors become well established, you will not use the same amount of treats as you once did, but you will still randomly reinforce. It's like when I was a kid: Every time I brushed my teeth or made my bed, I earned a sticker on my chart. Obviously, as a 30-year old I am no longer earning stickers for brushing my teeth. These types of behaviors have been engrained, and no longer needs that type of reinforcement. In fact, the behaviors in and of themselves have become reinforcing. The success experienced from performing the behavior becomes a reinforcement.

"Go to" Reinforcers

Again, during the process of training, *reinforcement is always chosen by the dog,* and the *reinforcement is always changing.* Within a three-minute training session, I may reward three pieces of chicken and a release to go sniff a mailbox. It all depends on what I notice my dog is interested in at the moment.

It's important to watch your dog to see what he wants at *a particular moment,* and use that desire to get what you want, and then give him what he wants. This idea is called the Premack Principle.

With the following types of reinforcers, you will release your dog with a *go* cue. For example, I see my dog really wants to go sniff a specific area of grass, but he's starting to pull. Great, so here is an excellent opportunity for training!

> **Other Examples of Reinforcers:**
>
> Sniffing an area of grass
> Chasing a leaf being blown in the wind
> Going to a person
> Chasing a squirrel
> A game of tug or tag

I will start moving toward the blade of grass, but I will only move forward when the leash is loose. As soon as we do get to the area with a loose leash, and this may take awhile, especially at first, then I will release him to what he finds rewarding with, "Okay, Boy, go sniff."

The idea of giving in to something that seems "naughty," like chasing a squirrel, almost seems backwards, but it works, and it is a good example of the Premack Principle in practice. One of my favorite trainers Kathy Sdao was sharing with us during a seminar about training dolphins. Kathy worked as a contractor with the military. She trained wild dolphins to detect mines in the ocean. There is a specific time of year when the whales would migrate in, and the dolphins loved to play on the waves these whales made. Kathy used the Premack Principle (Remember, you get what you want, and then give your dog what he wants). The dolphins that she was working with were wild and free, but even so, Kathy would get a behavior that she wanted from the dolphin and release the dolphin to go play.

This same principle can be used with the dreaded squirrel. Obviously, first making sure that both dog and squirrel are safe, you can "chase" a squirrel with a dog. When I've done this with dogs, we chase a couple feet, and usually within a few seconds, the squirrel is headed up a tree. This principle works.

I love using the Premack Principle because we can allow our dogs to pursue all of the so-called "naughty" behaviors that we tend to fight. For example, pulling on the leash to sniff a specific bush is something that we no longer have to fight. The trick is to use those "naughty" behaviors to your advantage. It's like finally giving in to the current of the river and just going with the flow. Nature is always going to win, so you might as well go with it and make it work for you.

Remember Reinforcement Makes Behavior Stronger
Reinforcement is very powerful - so powerful, in fact, that sometimes we inadvertently reinforce behaviors that we don't want without realizing it. Such may be the case with the *go to* reinforcement of sniffing a blade of grass. What did the behavior look like when I released my dog? Was he walking perfectly with the "J" shaped leash all the way to the grass, or was he slightly pulling the last three steps that were closest to the particular bade he was interested in? These details are pertinent to consider.

The reason this attention is pertinent is that it must be clearly understood that if we allow any sort of carelessness when leash walking (like releasing after he walked tight on the last three steps to the grass), then that's the behavior we are reinforcing and making stronger.

It's vital, just as we talked about, to be a defensive leash walker, and to be aware of your environment, of what you are reinforcing. If your dog pulls to get to a person, and you say, *"but he's fine once we get there,"* and allow your dog to pull, you have now reinforced pulling to get to people. The result is you have made this behavior stronger.

Approach your dog's desire to greet someone as a training opportunity. Get what you want, walking loosely on the leash, and give your dog what he wants, greeting the person. Then use your release, "Go see Aunt Jenny." You have now reinforced the behavior you wanted. At first, it will take more time. You may need to back up several times and restart, but your dog will begin to understand what he must do to get what he wants.

Reinforcement is the key to every behavior you want. Be a student of your dog and begin to look for things that HE (remember, not you) really enjoys, and use those things to your advantage.

Just as you focus on things your dog likes, you should also consider things that you do that he doesn't like.

For example, many times in my group class I see new handlers working on a cue who do something that is more reinforcing for them than for the dog. So the dog finally comes flying in for a fantastic recall (come), and the owner starts petting the dog all over his ears and head. In a few seconds the dog backs his entire body away from handler, trying to get the owner to stop petting. In the meantime, the owner is smiling and happy, but I can tell from the dog's body language that the owner's behavior wasn't effective in reinforcing the fantastic recall his dog had just performed. Petting the dog on the head wasn't reinforcing for him; instead, the pet owner was happy, and it reinforced him or her but not the dog.

Over all the years of training, I have only worked with one dog who enjoyed being petted more than receiving food or other reinforcers; that's how rare it is.

So besides being a student of your dog to see what he likes, be aware of how human you are and that there may be things that you are doing that are only a reinforcement in your own perception.

Reinforcement Exercises with Leash Walking
The next training secret makes all the difference in the world. In fact, when I did the exercise that I am about to share with you, I ended up teaching a heel with a *watch* behavior, a nice reward to get two positive behaviors for the price of one!

Reinforcing Eye Contact

For me, I feel the strongest foundation in leash walking is working on the eye contact. As I hope I have made clear by now, training is not just about your dog but about you as well. Are you both paying attention to each other?

Exercise 1) Once a day take your dog and a handful of treats and go to your front porch, driveway, or yard to train. Take one treat and place it between the thumb and pointer finger. Place the treat directly in front of your dog's nose, and draw the treat up to your face. While you are drawing the treat up, say slowly w-a-t-c-h. Draw your hand up to the side of your eyes. Look at your dog's eyes (if he allows). When your hand gets to the side of your cheek, say, "Good." Deliver the treat and repeat. Continue until you've finished your handful of pea-sized treats. Say your end cue and go back inside. An end cue is a cue that allows the dog to know that he is done with the training exercise and he is free to go. (An end cue will be used after every training session, for example *all done*, *finished*, or *that'll do*.) Repeat this exercise throughout the day as many times as you'd like. I practiced this exercise 1-3 times a day with my dogs to improve their leash walking skills.

Exercise 2) Another version of the distracted dog exercise (page 40) is to say your dog's name from time to time, and as soon as he turns to look at you, click and reinforce with a treat.

Exercise 3) When you walk the dog, take high level treats with you and a clicker. I want you to watch your dog's eyes. If he looks slightly in your direction, click and treat but continue walking. Do not stop to deliver the treat. Work on moving while you hand over the treat. Taking a bait bag on the walk can be helpful.

Caution: Bait bags cue a dog that it is time to train. Dogs may become conditioned to listen only when they see the bait bag which is not what you from your dog. I use bait bags sometimes, or I will use a baggy loaded with treats in my hooded sweatshirt pocket. I suggest changing it up; wear your bait bag one day and try a different approach the next.

Exercise 4) Every couple of weeks, go to a park with your dog and take along a blanket that you can both sit on. Be sure to take a stuffed Kong® or some sort of chewy that your dog enjoys. Watch your dog's eyes. Every time your dog looks at you, click (or mark) and give a *high* reward treat.

Consistency & Patience

Follow Through

I think we've all witnessed a situation at the grocery store with a mother telling her child something over and over. For example, a mother is shopping with her small child. Jimmy is standing in the cart, and Momma declares loudly enough for everyone to hear, "Jimmy, sit down." She continues with threats to Jimmy that if he doesn't sit, they will leave the store. After listening to her give Jimmy ten different threats, you yourself are ready to take Jimmy out of the store for Momma! Jimmy knew that she wasn't going to leave, so he continued with his behavior.

Dogs are like kids in that they need consistency. Even as adults we need consistency. We need to know the exact tasks our employer expects us to accomplish by a specific deadline. We would not appreciate our employer changing the deadline from day to day. Likewise, dogs want to know what is expected of them and when it is expected, and they thrive when the follow-through is consistent.

Consistent Cue

For instance, if you cue "sit" in a location when you feel your dog can successfully focus when you know he is paying attention, but he doesn't sit, you need to be consistent and follow through. There are times when Morgan decides she doesn't want to come inside late at night. If I know with certainty that she heard me when I called to her but she didn't come, I would start moving toward her to follow through, and within seconds she will come inside. When your dog does not respond to your cue, you must move off the couch, so to speak, and encourage the dog to follow through. Remember, unlike humans, dogs are not verbal; they read your body. You must use your body's movement at times to follow through.

Further, you must be consistent with your cueing. *Come* is *come*; it's not *come here* or *come on!* or *come, come, come!* The cue is simply "come."

Catch All Good Things

When you turn on the news, is it ever good news? I think that we can all agree that within our human nature, we tend to naturally focus on the negatives. This concept rings true for our dogs as well. Here's a good example: Your puppy is sitting beautifully next to you while you are watching your favorite TV show. He is chewing on his Kong®, and your focus is on your show. Soon, he gets up and finds his ball, brings it to you in the living room, and begins barking, inviting you to play. You immediately pause the TV show and give him all the attention in the world. Yes, you reinforced the barking. It's important to change your focus, to purposefully reinforce the behaviors that you want, point them out happily, and applaud your dog for the desired behaviors. Look for moments and opportunities to give your dog a "That-a- boy!"

Pop Quiz!!
Real Life Scenario Examples: How to Respond
1) You go to the backyard, and your dog excitably jumps on you.
2) You sit down on the couch to watch TV, and your dog walks over and pushes his head under your hand.
3) Your dog barks at you for supper.
4) When on a walk you with you, your dog starts pulling towards a telephone pole.

Appropriate responses:
1) You could
a. completely leave the backyard
b. cue a sit and see if he responds. If he does, praise and throw his tennis ball (be sure there's not a pattern of jump and then sit)
c. completely ignore him and once he's settled, you give attention

2) You could
a. nonchalantly move your hand away from your dog and continue watching TV
b. remove your hand, wait a few seconds and ask for a sit or another behavior and then initiate petting.

3) You could ignore him by leaving the room, wait a few seconds, and return to the room. Wait until later (15 minutes is acceptable) to feed him.

4) You could back up and start moving forward. Every time there is tension on the leash back up again. Don't allow sniffing until you get there on a loose leash.

Reinforcement
Though at this point it may seem there is a lot to know and do to be successful in training your dog for the leash walking experience, I assure you that you will be well rewarded for your efforts. Reinforcement is just another step to help you accomplish your goal.

CHAPTER 8

MICHELLE'S SECRET: LET'S GO

I suggest to all of my students that they start teaching the cue *let's go* before starting the heel exercises. Heel is such a difficult behavior to teach, so establishing a strong *let's go* greatly aids the process of teaching heel.

After trying every single "positive" method under the sun I have designed my own method for the *let's go* cue. I think that you will enjoy this method and find success with it as my students have throughout the years.

Here are a few pointers before you start training the *let's go* cue:

Pointer One: Be consistent. It's worthwhile to remember that allowing leash pulling only serves to reinforce the behavior. I remember walking my own dog and realizing three minutes into the walk that I had been following my dog as he happily forged in front of me pulling at the end of the leash.

I would have a nice bank account if I had a $1 for every time I've heard a student say, "Michelle, she stops pulling once she gets to _____ (fill in the blank). Yes, I am sure she does! Let's think about pulling for a moment. A dog does what works for him (Humans do too!). So, by allowing the dog to pull, the handler enables the dog to get the desired object, and the *owner reinforces the unwanted behavior!*

Stay alert and aware as a handler if your dog is pulling.

Pointer Two: **Be aware of tension in your body.** When I hand the leash over to the owner as we are talking about leash walking, I often watch the owner become visibly tense and wrap the leash ten times around his arm and hand. That's a good sign this owner has had some pretty rough experiences with the dog on the leash. The owner has been conditioned to react this way. As handlers you need to realize that, when your body is tense, your dog will feed off of that.

As you are leash walking, breathe, stay loose, and know you are in control.

Dogs can pick up on the slightest tension of their owner. Whether it's as severe as wrapping the leash several times around your arm, or a slight tension of pulling back on leash, your dog will pick up on your body tension.

As you are leash walking, focus on your body, breathe, and be aware of any tension in your muscles.

Challenge for you: When you first start the *let's go* exercise, try wearing a belt around your waist with the leash handle looped through at least once because this formation will allow you to realize how much you are using your arms to pull your dog into position. I didn't realize the degree to which my dog was pulling until I walked with the leash on a belt, and every pet owner I have worked with says the same thing. During this exercise, you must resist using your hands and arms. Even though the leash will be on your waist, you will continually try reaching for the leash, but *hands off* at least for now.

Second, as previously mentioned, when dogs pull, we naturally pull back creating a bad cycle. We want to help the dog to overcome his natural reflex of pulling forward as we pull backwards. I have also found that dogs become used to feeling pressure and keep applying pressure when walked by owners who unknowingly reinforced it. Perhaps from the dog's point of view that's how walking on a leash is "supposed to feel."

Next, when the dog pulls, our arm extends giving them even more pull room. It has been my observation from watching pet owners and even myself that our tendency is to move our arm while holding the leash to pull our dog into position and not move our bodies at all. You will apply the "whole body" principle in my technique explained in this chapter.

Finally, as humans we communicate with our arms and hands all the time. As we are pointing with our finger and motioning with our arm, we will say, "Could you please move over there?". *A dog looks at your body as a whole to understand what you are communicating.* So when you want the dog to move in a specific direction, you should move your entire body. In this chapter you are going to learn how to use your body to communicate successful leash walking.

Understand Movement

As noted earlier, dogs understand movement much differently than humans. If you have ever watched herding breeds, they will move in the direction that they want the sheep to go. Have you ever noticed when you start to walk toward your dog, unlike a human, he will back up? Using this principle in leash walking, you will move in the direction that you want your dog to go.

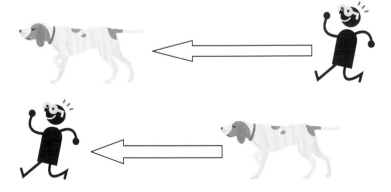

Dogs understand movement of *our body as a whole*. Apply this understanding when you want your dog to get up off the couch. Instead of pulling him by the collar, try using the movement of your body. Move in the direction that you would like him to go and you can always pat your leg to encourage him. This strategy would mean that you would turn your back toward your dog and walk away. Make sure when he gets down that you praise.

Now we are ready to begin the let's go! cue.

You will need treats, clicker, leash, dog, and bait bag (treat tote).

For your first few times working on this, I would like you to take the leash handle with your dominant hand and place your hand with the leash against your tummy (with hand flat against tummy, pressing the leash against your tummy as shown in the picture on the next page). This position will help you realize how much you are using your arms versus your body as a whole to get your dog into position.

Steps with "Let's Go"

1) Start walking.
2) If your dog moves out in front of you, stop and make a sound with your voice or kissy sound with your lips. The sound that you make is to let your dog know you will be moving in a different direction. The sound is a matter of choice but should be consistent.
3) Start backing up until your dog is behind you or at your side.
4) When he's behind or beside you click or mark, and quickly move forward again.
5) During this entire process, any time your dog walks two or more steps alongside you, click, and deliver a treat. I give my dogs a lot of verbal feedback and praise.

Please note: It's crucial when you are going through this entire process that you go through the steps quickly. Don't wait for him to look; simply go through the process. He will look at you once the movement begins.

Step One: Start walking.

As you are moving forward, observe your dog. If you get one to two steps with your dog at your side, fantastic! Click and deliver treats, but make sure you keep walking. Please do not stop and ask for a sit as you deliver a treat, and then move on. It is completely fine to slow way down especially at first while you get the hang of it to deliver the treat, but please continue the movement.

Photo by Bryan Huntting

Also, be *watching your dog for any intention of moving out in front* of you.

Step Two: (If dog goes out in front of you), stop and make a sound. The sole purpose of this sound is to be polite. When I was pregnant, I had gotten so dehydrated that I was admitted to the hospital for fluids. The nurse was taking me down a hall as I was attached to the IV pole. She turned to go in a different direction without saying a word to me as I continued walking forward. I quickly changed directions, but in that moment, I thought, "Wow that must be how dogs feel when they are on leash and no one alerts them of a change." It has been my experience that a sound gives a polite "heads up" that we're moving or changing direction. Again, this sound should not be correctional, but a polite sound to let him know you are changing directions. Sometimes I use a quick "kissing" sound, and I have also used a quick "hup" sound.

Photo by Bryan Huntting

Michelle stopped because Boy went out in front of her. She made a sound and started moving back.

Step Three: Start backing up until your dog is behind you or at your side.

Photo by Bryan Huntting

It is important to make sure that he is actually beside you or behind you. Many new handlers think that right in front of them is okay and reinforce this position. Right in front is not beside or behind. Further, do not stand and wait for your dog to look at you before backing up. This is the opposite of what you should do. Instead, I want you to start moving in the direction you want him to go. Once you do, he will look at you.

Michelle will keep moving back until Boy is beside her or behind her.

Photo by Bryan Huntting

Step Four: When he's behind or beside you, click and quickly move forward again.

Boy is behind Michelle, so she clicks and moves forward. Note: With this method, at times when moving forward, you will need to shift the leash around your back to the front of your body again.

The reward in this situation is the movement forward, not a treat. If you treat for this exercise, your dog will more than likely learn the pattern of going out to the end of the leash and return for a tasty treat, then repeat by going back out to the end of the leash.

Photo by Bryan Huntting

Step Five: During this entire process, any time your dog walks two or more steps alongside you, click (or mark), and deliver a treat. Again, do not stop walking when delivering the treat, and never cue a sit when you are working on leash walking! Expect that it will take some practice to learn how to keep moving while you hand the treat to your dog, but I know you can do it. Watch your dog for ANY eye contact toward you; then click and treat.

Photo by Bryan Huntting

I give my dogs a lot of feedback, praise, and verbal communication during leash walking. Remember, this is a dance, a two-way street, and communication is important. I don't want to overdo it, but offer enough to give them confidence. I think you can relate to this; need for reinforcement especially when trying something new. We want to hear feedback from our instructor or teacher that we are on the right track during the process of learning. However, recognize that giving sufficient feedback is different from continuous talking. I think we've all spent time with someone who was way too chatty. What was your reaction to that person? I have a hard time concentrating after a while and shut down while I try to say the occasional, "Uh huh." I have observed dogs do something similar when they've been with an overly chatty handler. People don't enjoy it, and I've observed dogs really don't enjoy it either. This is the time to focus on behavior, and give good constructive criticisms and praise to your dog during the training process.

Leash Walking Gear

Photo by Cheryl Kenyon

I like using a belt with the handle of the leash drawn through the belt and then attached around my waist. Being tethered to your dog in this manner allows you to use your entire body to move in the direction that you want your dog to go.

I have tried several different belts, and found the one that works well for me is the Rigger's® belt. I have had other belts break with a hard pulling dog. You can find these belts at any military surplus or ww.amazon.com.

Photo by Cheryl Kenyon

Using the treat tote is not common for me as a trainer because, as mentioned earlier, the bag itself can become a cue to the dog that it's time to work, and therefore, when the bait bag is off, he fails to perform. However, during the beginning of the leash walking training, using the bait bag is the easiest way for the handler to manage everything. Eventually, in one or more months, you will want to begin to fade out using the treat pouch. A nice transition could be a Lickety Stik® to use as the treat, which allows your dog to quickly lick while walking. These sticks are also a great treat for dogs that tend to have a "hard mouth" (take treats hard) on a walk due to arousal.

Step One: Walk with Dog

Photo by Bryan Huntting

Tip: Keep this process at a snappy pace. Be sure that you aren't backing up slowly. This process should be done in a quick, graceful movement.

Step Two: Boy is out in front of Michelle, so Michelle stops.

Photo by Bryan Huntting

Step Three: Michelle makes her sound to get Boy's attention and starts moving back.

Photo by Bryan Huntting

Step Four: Michelle moves back until Boy is behind her. As soon as he is behind Michelle, she will click and move forward.

Photo by Bryan Huntting

Step Five: Boy stays beside Michelle more than two steps so Michelle clicks and delivers a treat.

Photo by Bryan Huntting

As long as Boy stays by Michelle every few steps, she clicks and delivers treats. Remember to keep moving while delivering treats.

Photo by Bryan Huntting

Photo by Bryan Huntting

Do you see the nice "J" shape with the leash? This is what you should strive for and reward when walking your dog.

Here is another example of a "J" shape in the leash:

Photo by Cheryl Kenyon

Here are Michelle and Boy taking you through the steps again.

When you see your dog has the *intention* of pulling, stop and make your sound. In other words, don't wait to stop walking when he's five steps ahead. Go ahead and start the process of *let's go* if he is about to move out in front of you. When backing up, don't wait for him to stop or even look at you; just start moving back.

Remember, it is more effective to simply start backing up even if the dog isn't looking. You are then using your entire body to communicate in a way that your dog understands. Your dog will learn you would like him to move in that particular direction.

Photo by Bryan Huntting

In the photo above, Boy is walking out in front of Michelle, so Michelle has made a sound and started walking back.

Photo by Bryan Huntting

In the photo above, Michelle is walking back until Boy is at her side.

Photo by Bryan Huntting

In the above photo, Boy has come to Michelle's side, and Michelle clicked (or marked). She did not treat, and they are now moving forward.

Photo by Bryan Huntting

Photo by Bryan Huntting

Boy is walking alongside Michelle for many steps, and he is getting verbal praise.

Photo by Bryan Huntting

Michelle and Boy are demonstrating ideal form of polite leash walking in the above photo.

Before You Start the Method

Often times, I recommend that students practice the steps with a human at first to work on the mechanics of this method. You practice being the handler for this practice session and have a human assistant that will hold the end of the leash as you practice the steps. Tell the human to go out in front of you as the dog would. I know it may seem silly, but it can help you practice how to move so that doing the movement with your dog will be a little easier.

Lack of Movement

When I stop walking, it has become a cue to my dogs to check in with me. Sometimes their nose leads them away from me, and, I stop my movement, they realize, "Huh? Oh yes, I need to get back beside mom."

Again, be sure to start off with short training time periods (starting from five-minutes increments) so you don't get frustrated. In the meantime, you can use training tools for your every-day exercise time to ensure your dog is not pulling you and getting reinforcement for doing so.

Advanced Let's Go: Taking it to the next level

Once your dog understands that when you stop moving he should come back quickly to your side, you can then begin working on more advanced skills. I strongly suggest practicing these skills with the belt at first so that your hands will be free to continue moving while you are clicking and reinforcing. Eye contact is crucial. Your dog walking next to you as he watches your eyes is a fantastic accomplishment. To achieve this objective, anytime your dog looks up toward you facial area or even does a quick flick of the eye over toward the area of your body, you can click and treat this behavior. Just as before, when you deliver the treat, it's important to continue walking. Again, do not stop walking after you click or ask for a sit. If you do stop, cue a "sit," and then deliver a treat, your dog will become confused and not understand the expectation.

Note: My hand positions on the leash are different when I am using treats. I tend to hold the leash with only one hand to free my other hand for treat delivery.

Photo by Cheryl Kenyon

When Boy walks five steps beside or behind Michelle, she gives him a click.

126

Photo by Cheryl Kenyon

When Boy looks up at Michelle, she gives a click and treat.

Photo by Cheryl Kenyon

Michelle and Boy are still moving when Michelle reaches for a treat.

Photo by Cheryl Kenyon

Michelle and Boy are still moving as she delivers the treat.

Position When Delivering the Treat

Just as timing with treat delivery is important, so is the position of the dog when teaching polite leash walking. I have often seen a dog on leash walk a few nice steps alongside the handler, and then the handler cues a "sit" to deliver the treat. Avoid ever cueing a sit when training and reinforcing polite leash walking.

Delivering a treat while moving

- Will provide more reinforcement in a shorter period of time
- Will reinforce the behavior as it is happening rather than reinforcing a different behavior (like sit)

To watch a demo video of me doing the *let's go* exercise visit,

www.michellehuntting.com/demo.html

Following and practicing the method I have described for you in this chapter will set both owner and dog up for successful leash walking and ultimately make for a pleasurable experience for them both.

CHAPTER 9

HANDLING SKILLS

The next topic for discussion is horses. I know, right? A discussion about horses in a book on leash walking seems out of place, but there are many similarities that we can learn to apply in dog training. I was working for a client of mine who is a breeder of Great Danes, but also trains horses. She had her sons with us during our session as we were teaching polite leash walking to one of her Great Danes. I handed the leash over to one of the sons. With much effort, he tried to move his Great Dane's body into position. After watching him struggle I asked his mom, "What did I just do to get her into position?" I took the leash again and moved the Great Dane into position. The mom said to me, "Michelle that is exactly how we move our horses when we want to get them into position." Once we explained this to her son, he was able to successfully move his full-sized Great Dane into position.

I have never trained horses, so the common trait was a new idea to me. When I went home, I started thinking over this similarity when a light bulb came on in my head. I asked my friend if I could borrow her horse training manuals to read what they said about handling. I am still completely floored how similar horse handling skills are in to dog handling skills.

This discovery led me to more research and another visit to my client's house. This time I was there to see the horses, not the dogs. I met the grandmother who also trains horses and observed her work with the horses. I received a lesson. It was great fun, and I am grateful to them for opening their home to me and also to my friend, Miranda Vallade, who took the photos for this chapter.

Photo by Miranda Vallade

I observed great handling skills that could improve canine leash walking skills. Horse trainers use the reigns, their body, their energy, and words to constantly communicate to the horse. If we apply the handling skills I observed trainers used with horses, we could obtain the desired leash walking skills with our dogs. Using the same principles, I am able to walk all three of my dogs on separate leashes and communicate to them individually with slight movements on the leash, as well as my body and my voice.

Holding the Leash

Any horse handler would tell you that coiling the reins of the bridle is a poor way of communicating. Holding the reins in this manner would be like trying to share an extremely important message through an insulated wall. When you open up the leash so it's flat in your hand, you are able to clearly communicate and give direction.

As I mentioned before, I know a student is tense when I see him wrap the leash around his hand numerous times before we start walking his dog. I understand he's nervous because of bad experiences in the past, but coiling the leash around your hand is not safe. If, for whatever reason, your dog were to take off on you, the coil that you wrapped around your hand will tighten and possibly cause injury.

It's important the handler is holding the leash in a way that promotes control and communication and to work toward helping the dog begin to think through his arousal as I mentioned the wave-like pattern in the previous chapter (page 45).

Photo by Miranda Vallade

In the photo, Jennifer is demonstrating an example of coiling. Do NOT do this!! This hold will not gain the optimal communication with the leash, and it puts you at risk for injury.

When holding the leash, keep your hands relaxed around the leash and slightly open. The optimal communication happens when the leash is flat. If I am walking all three of my dogs, I never put my hand inside the handle. I always come in on (shorten) the leash and have each leash positioned in a different place so I can communicate individually to each dog.

Slight Pressure on Leash
In nearly ten years of working with dogs, I have used different

methods and also observed many other people working with their dogs. I have noticed things that we do that are effective and other things that we continually do even though ineffective.

I have observed leash popping to be ineffective. Leash popping occurs when the handler quickly jerks the leash as a correction. I have observed this form of correction does very little in communicating a desired behavior or to stop an undesired behavior. On the other hand, I have found the elimination of pressure on the leash is very effective. I have also found that using slight pressure and releasing pressure communicates the behavior I would like from my dog. During my horse lesson, I discovered that horse trainers effectively use the same method. Clearly, this strategy is easier on the dog's neck as well.

Using Your Body
As detailed before, dogs understand movement of our body. By using our body movement, we can control where our dogs move. These movements are sometimes minuscule, but they may also be very noticeable. I am amazed at the similarities of how horse trainers use their bodies in the same way that I have observed skilled dog handlers use their bodies. Obviously there are minor differences due to the size difference of the species.

I use the bend of my knee, the slight leaning forward of my body, or the movement of my body as a whole to communicate to my dog the exact position that I want, and he is able to understand quite well through these positions and movements. Later in this chapter, there are several photos of me demonstrating the use of my body to communicate to my dog.

Though it seems unnatural to use our whole body because we are naturally prone to use our hands or our arms to communicate to our dog or to move the dog into position, for a dog, the use of our arms means something completely different than what we are trying to communicate. As earlier noted, hands are a far less effective tool than using legs or hips. Patricia McConnell gives the reasons why we have a tendency to use our arms and how the dogs perceive this behavior.

What is natural to all primates, including us, is to push others away with our hands (or forepaws). But to a dog, a raised paw can signify submission or a request to play or the beginning of a dominance-related mount, but it never seems to mean 'go away.' [McConnell, Patricia, On the Other End of the Leash 27]

Using Your Voice

The sounds that we make communicate to dogs what we want. Horse trainers make a sound with the side of their mouth to encourage movement forward, and I make a similar sound with my dogs.

When I read Patricia McConnell's book *The Other End of the Leash*, I was fascinated with the research that she had conducted on sound for her doctoral study. Particularly fascinating to me was her discussion of the sounds trainers (no matter what language they spoke) made to get their horse or dog to stop, or move forward.

...Peruvian Quechua sheepdog handlers used short, repeated whistles and words to encourage their dogs to get moving. English-speaking sled dog racers belted out short, repeated sounds—words like 'Go! Go! Go!' and 'Hike! Hike! Hike!' and 'Hyah! Hyah!'—to encourage more speed from their dogs. In contrast, when handlers wanted to slow or stop an animal, they used one single, continuous note... Common English 'slow down' signals to dogs and horses are 'Stay,' 'whoa,' and 'easy'. [McConnell, Patricia, The Other End of the Leash 57]

The tone of voice is also an effective tool to communicate to your dog to speed up if he's going slower than you like or to slow down if he's going too fast. The risk, however, is that you may inadvertently use your tone of voice to cause your dog to become overly excited if you are anxious. When I am working on getting my dogs to calm down, I will speak a slower, lower-toned voice, drawing my words out like "Gooooood Boy." If an owner is anxious and begins chanting in a choppy "Good Boy! Good Boy! Good Boy!" then this rhythm is similar to the one used to encourage dogs to speed up. Generally, when I hear owners say cues or reinforcement repetitively in that way, they are usually using a higher pitched, excited voice. The dog that may already be overly stimulated then goes through the roof. The sounds you make and the tone you use are extremely important when training. Again, it's not necessarily what you say but how you say it. Start becoming aware of how you speak to your dog. If you notice that he is getting overly aroused, you can stop and ask yourself, "Why?" "What's going on in the environment?" "How have I been using my voice?"

My Day with the Horses

So, after a little persuasion, I took a horse for a walk around the pasture to see how it felt. Surprisingly, it felt very natural even though I had never led a horse in my entire life. It was very much like the handling skills I use in walking a dog, a very large dog. As I watched the handlers interact with the horses, I was still floored by the similarities between good handling skills with dogs and horses. As dog owners, we become frustrated when our methods of communication are on the wrong frequency. Our natural tendency, as I noted before, is to move dogs with our hands and arms, a task which would be completely impossible with horses. We cannot reposition a horse by lifting his legs and moving him, as I see dog owners do. If good handling skills are applied with effective use of voice, body, and leash pressure, pet owners will begin to see the response on the leash that they greatly desire from their pet. I have included pictures of me leading a horse and a veteran horse handler leading the horse to compare to photos of me handling dogs.

Photos by Miranda Vallade

Notice my body moving forward in the direction of desired movement. I am not as relaxed as I normally would be because I am inexperience with horses. The horse is much bigger in person and a little intimidating to me, so I am holding the lead firmly!

Turn with Dog

Photos by Miranda Vallade

Above, Michelle is demonstrating a turn with Boy. Note how lightly Michelle is holding the leash. Her hand is not through the handle. Both hands are open and relaxed, and her leash is flat. Michelle is communicating with her body during the turn by slight leans and bends of her hips and legs. Michelle also communicates verbally to her dog right before she plans on turning. Michelle verbally gets Boy's attention as well.

Photo by Miranda Vallade

Notice the handler is moving his body into the desired area of movement. He is moving the horse into a right turn. Hands on the lead are relaxed.

Photo by Miranda Vallade

Notice the handler is using body, moving into the horse for the turn.

Photo by Miranda Vallade

Photo by Miranda Vallade

In the photo above, Michelle is dramatizing the movements that she makes with the leash with the intention of showing what the leash looks like when she wants her dog to move forward. Michelle is right handed, so she lightly holds the leash in her right hand (not through the handle), and with her left hand, she pushes forward to communicate to her dog that they are moving forward as she takes a step with her left foot at the same time.

Photo by Miranda Vallade

The handler is moving forward with the lead.

Photo by Miranda Vallade

The pictures demonstrate a good example of how to hold the leash on a walk. Notice that Michelle does not have her right hand in the handle and how light her left hand is on the leash.

Photo by Miranda Vallade

In the picture above, Michelle is using her body to communicate to Boy that she wants him to move back. It was pretty adorable. Notice how Michelle's knees are bent. Michelle moved her left leg out to slightly align him just by using the movement of her body. Michelle is walking into him as well as saying "back" and using her hand motion for "back."

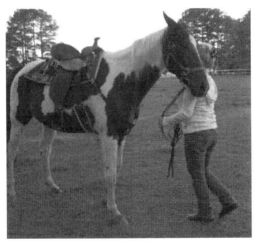

Photo by Miranda Vallade

The above picture demonstrates the horse handler backing her horse by using her body pressure, voice, and leash.

Photo A   *Photo B*

In photo A, Boy is starting to pull out in front of Michelle. You can see in Photo A, Michelle starts applying gentle pressure back, and in Photo B, Michelle continues applying pressure until he moves into position. As soon as he does, Michelle releases pressure. During the movements, Michelle would also cue "w-h-o-a" or "slow down." The handler below is moving back on the lead for a stop.

Though the relationship between training a horse and a dog may seem farfetched, anyone who has ever done both, and done them effectively, can readily recognize the similarities. Both species rely on body movement, proper use of voice, and appropriate technique of holding the leash or lead. Common sense tells us that these handling skills are imperative with horses because of their size, but we can apply that same common sense to handling our dogs.

CHAPTER 10

HEEL

So now that you have learned about how to use your body, voice, energy, and handling skills, and your dog has learned calming skills, impulse control, and *let's go*, you are ready to learn heel. Heel is one of the last behaviors that I establish when teaching polite leash walking.

When you are training heel, you will not put your hand in the handle because you will often use leash pressure and movements with the leash to help your dog get into position with your left hand. It's important to consider which leash is the right one for you. As noted earlier, I prefer a leather leash because it enables me to communicate effectively with the dog. (See chapter 2 for discussion on various leashes that are available.)

Time in Training
When training heel, I plan eight weeks of training sessions, five days a week, 15-minutes per day. The 15-minute sessions should be spread out through the day with three, five-minute sessions or less. It is more beneficial to your dog to have several focused sessions than one long unfocused session. When teaching the positioning of heel, you can choose one of two options of methods: leash pressure or targeting.

Luring in the training context, is using a treat to move your dog into the precise position that you'd like. Think of your treat as a magnet and your dog as the opposite attracted magnet. Wherever you move the treat, his nose will follow. If you have never used a treat as a lure, you may want to practice with a simple sit behavior before you start training heel.

Lure a Sit
Hold a treat between your thumb and index finger directly above your dog's nose. Hold the treat slightly up, as you move the treat slowly, encouraging your dog to move his head up which makes his bottom go down. When you move the treat up, do so in an upward slow movement, but your treat should stay directly in front of your dog's nose. Be sure not to move the treat too high. If your dog is jumping, this is a good indicator that you moved the treat up too high.

Photos taken by author

Now that you've had some practice using a lure with sit, you are ready to lure the heel behavior. Heel is a little more complex with luring and will require some skills as a handler. You will use your own body movement as well as the lure.

The one caution that I have with this method is to quickly fade the lure. In other words, once you've taken the dog through the steps of the exercise a few times, then you will use your hand without a treat, adding a cue word association. Soon, you will move to using a word only to cue the behavior.

Step 1a

Start the training session with your dog sitting in front of you. This position may be the easiest for new handlers. Hold the lure (treat) with your left hand in front of his nose. You will be moving your treat in a "u" movement. The "u" begins with luring your dog that is in the sit position in front of you around behind you and then back and aligned with your left side. As you are luring the dog along your left side, you step back with your left foot as this movement helps the dog understand what you expect from him from your body movement. When you have lured your dog around your back, you will move your left foot back up beside your stationary right foot as your dog positions on your left side. When your dog is positioned at your left leg, you will move the treat up to encourage your dog to sit.

Luring for Heel Position

Photos by author   *Step 1*   *Step 2*

(1) Start with the treat in front of your dog's nose.
(2) Move the treat back.

Step 3   Step 4

(3) As you move the treat back, move your left leg back as well.

(4) Lure your dog back and using a lure, encourage your dog to turn around to face in the same position as you. As you are turning, also move your leg back into alignment with your right foot.

(5) When your dog is alongside you, move the treat up to encourage a sit.

The diagram demonstrates the movement of your treat. Starting with the dog in front of the handler, the handler will move the lure arcing around, moving almost behind the body, and then up to encourage a sit.

Photo by author   Step 5

You will work on step one for four days or until it is fluid for both you and your dog. After several sessions, you will fade (remove) the lure and once dog is in a heel position deliver treat. After day three, rather than giving a treat you will praise for sitting next to you.

Step 1b
You want to help your dog gain a positive association with the left side. Once you've positioned him into a sit at your left side, you will praise and treat. During this time, encourage and reinforce him to maintain eye contact. Do this step once a day for four days.

Leash Pressure
Personally, I find the leash a positive way of communicating with my dog, similar to training a horse with reins. One man is able to control a very large animal by the movement of the leather reins. As a humane, "positive" handler, you can have the same ability, without pain or force, to communicate very easily with your dog on the leash.

Leash pressure requires using a technique of pressure, release, and leash movement to communicate the direction that you'd like your dog to go. There is an art to learning how to do this technique, so be patient with yourself and practice. Note: The pressure is so gentle and slight that someone observing would have to watch closely. I never use a leash correction like a "pop" (quick jerk to the leash) or holding the dog up in the air with my techniques. This type of training style has been proven to cause harm emotionally, and potentially physically as well to a dog, so please refrain as this will only set you back in your training goals. When you are training, your dog needs to wear a flat collar. This exercise is not intended for petite breeds or dogs with a sensitive neck. Please see chapter 13 for specific heel exercises for petite breeds.

As a handler, you should be aware of your dog's movement and in tune with which way to add pressure, when to release, and when to change direction as you work together as a team. It's important to praise and talk to your dog through this entire process. Remember, when you do talk to your dog, do not use a high-pitched voice as this will only excite your dog and hinder your progress toward your training goal, a strong heel. I had a student in my leash-walking class once who talked to her dog in a high-pitched voice during the entire one-hour class. Once I called her attention to her tone, she changed and was amazed by how much better the dog listened and learned the behavior.

When you train heel, there are many different exercises to start individually, and after your dog masters each exercise individually you will begin to add the elements together.

Sit on Left Side with Leash Pressure

Reinforcing your dog for sitting at your left side is very important. With your dog on you left side, you will move in on your leash so that your dog has fewer options of movement. With him on your left side say "sit" and gently move the leash back and up, maintaining the gentle pressure until he sits. When he sits, quickly release the pressure, praise, and treat.

Photos by Miranda Vallade

Cue "sit" after the step and place gentle pressure on the leash to encourage the sit position. As his bottom touches the floor, release all pressure on the leash. Give your dog a lot of praise and a treat.

Photo by Bryan Huntting

Photo by Bryan Huntting

Moving Forward

When training leash pressure to move him forward, you will gently push the leash forward as you start moving and then release the leash pressure.

Photo by Miranda Vallade

Step 2: One Step

Once your dog is happy to be on your left side, get his attention by asking, "You ready?"

Photo by Bryan Huntting

Photo by Bryan Huntting

Now that you have your dog's attention, take a step forward with your LEFT foot while simultaneously moving forward with gentle pressure on the leash. Be sure that your hand is flat against the leash in a forward direction (as shown in the picture above) or very relaxed around the leash. Practice step 2 for one week. Do not move more than one step forward at this point.

Step 3: Adding More Steps

Now you will begin to add two to three steps for the heel. Before your last step, verbally cue "sit" before you actually stop walking to communicate to your dog that you plan to stop. Once you stop walking, apply gentle pressure until he places his bottom onto the ground. Once he does, release the pressure, praise, and treat.

In the photo above, Michelle is moving forward on the leash and starting with her left foot for heel.

In the photo, Michelle is taking three steps forward with relaxed hand positions on the leash.

Photo by Bryan Huntting

Michelle is about to stop so Michelle cue Boy to "sit."

Photo by Bryan Huntting

Michelle stop and applied gentle pressure on leash (only when needed). In this case Boy immediately sat for Michelle.

Once your dog is successfully able to maintain focus with three steps, you can slowly begin to add more steps. I would encourage you to begin to vary the number of steps too. So, for example, one time you will take four steps and cue a "sit," then six steps and cue a "sit," and then two steps and cue a "sit." It's important that you have your dog's focused attention before moving on to in the training process. Once you've successfully gained 10 or more focused steps, you can start marking (or clicking) and treating him for glancing at you. Be sure to watch for and click even a fast look in your location. When you deliver the treat, make sure that you do not stop walking.

Stop or Slow Down

When training a *stop*, begin to slow down with leash pressure; then, gently move the leash back, and say, "stand stay." The *stand stay* exercise is on page 181.

To help your dog slow down, as you slow down your pace, gently pull back and say the cue "e-a-s-y" or "w-o-a-h" drawn out in a soft, low tone.

Photo by Miranda Vallade

Right Turns

My personal preference is to have a tight turn when I walk my dogs. In addition to simply preferring to have my dogs close to me, there have been many circumstances when a close position has kept the dogs focused on me rather than a nearby dog or an object that I don't want them to get close to.

How to Teach Right Turns

1. Start this exercise with your dog seated on your left side.
2. Hold a treat directly in front of your dog's nose as you turn.
3. When you finish the turn, continue to lure your dog by moving the treat up into the air to encourage a sit. Once he sits, deliver the treat.

*Instead of using a treat, you can use a target stick to teach this behavior.

You are welcome to use leash pressure, but I have found that by the time I'm training turns with the dog, he is already reinforced to sit and move to the left side. However, if you do need to use leash pressure along with the treat, gently move the leash forward toward your dog's head as you turn to the right in a half circle and then move the leash upward and back to cue the "sit." As always, be sure to smile, talk, and praise your dog during this process.

Practice turn sessions separately from heel sessions. I suggest training one-minute sessions, three sessions per day for four days. When your dog is doing well and is moving with ease, then start adding right turns into your heel sessions.

Pictures Demonstrating Leash Pressure for Right Turn

Michelle is demonstrating moving the leash forward as Boy and she moves into the turn.

Michelle is moving Boy forward with the leash as they move around in the turn. Please note how far up on the leash her hand is. This position allows for more control and a tighter turn. If you are holding the leash by the handle, you will not have a tight turn.

Photo by Bryan Huntting

Boy is close to Michelle during the turn.

Photo by Bryan Huntting

Michelle is moving the leash back after they finish the turn to encourage a sit.

Left Turns

Left Turns. Left turns require little strategy or effort because you simply hold the leash in the same position, and you are the one that moves. There is no need to target or lure with the left turn.

Boy and Michelle walking in a heel position.

Target Training with Heel

If you have a sniffer, like my Bloodhound, or a timid dog, you will want to try target training. It is a great way to teach confidence with a heel, and to promote left-side position, and focus. I do not think that target training is required for every dog, but it is a good tool to use if this scenario is appropriate for you and your dog.

I like to teach target training for heel with my hand and also an object. If you have a petite breed, remember to use a long target stick. Your target object can be as simple as a rubber scraper or spatula from your kitchen. You could buy one of the fancy target sticks on the market, or make your own from a dowel, adding a fun smiley-faced ping pong ball on end. To view a demo video of me teaching heel, visit, www.michellehuntting.com/demo.html

In addition, handlers who wish to use the target stick as a training tool may refer to chapter 6 for a complete discussion.

In the pictures below I am demonstrating how to incorporate target training to teach heel.

Photo by Cheryl Kenyon

When you are teaching heel with the target stick, be sure to present the target stick every few steps, and based upon your dog's level of focus, gradually increase the number of steps before presenting the target stick.

Photo by Cheryl Kenyon

Photo by Cheryl Kenyon

Targeting for right turn

Targeting for a tighter right turn

Heel may very well be one of the more challenging training techniques you are called upon to master, but following one of the recommended strategies and working on them consistently and patiently will ultimately reap rewards for both you and your dog.

CHAPTER 11

TRAINING WHEELS

Tools help us get where we need to be. It's okay while you are in the process of training to use tools. Imagine if I made my three-year old ride his bike with no training wheels. This idea seems a bit silly as I know he probably doesn't have the coordination skills at this point to ride the bike, so in the meantime, I am going to allow the three-year old to get a "feel" of what it's like to successfully ride a bike. Obviously a ten-year old boy would never want to be seen riding a bike with training wheels because not only would he feel foolish, but with practice, he outgrew the need for this tool.

At this point in your training endeavors, you may wish to consider that you are the younger child on the bike. Until you have reached the experienced stage, consider using the tools that I have listed in this chapter to help set you and your dog up for success when you are on daily walks. During the formal training sessions, however, I would encourage you not to use a tool unless absolutely necessary. Using the tools outside of training sessions will allow you to reinforce the correct behaviors. Every dog is different so it's important to try the tools that suit you and your dog the best.

Head Halters

Gentle Leader® The Gentle Leader® wraps around the dog's nose and neck. The leash attaches under the dog's mouth so when the dog pulls, it self-corrects by turning the dog's head back towards you. It's important when fitting the halter that the strap that goes around the dog's neck is tight enough for you to only fit one finger underneath. The strap that goes over the dog's nose should be loose enough for you to pull down to the top of the dog's nose. He should not be able to pull it off. Please be careful with the Gentle Leader® as the halter will self correct, turning the dog's neck back so that hard pressure from you is unnecessary and dangerous to your dog. You want to be sure as a handler that the dog doesn't injure himself. You want to avoid any hard corrections as you use your good handling skills.

Canny Collar® These head halters have become one of my favorite tools for hard pullers, but when dogs have a tendency to lunge as my Bloodhound did in early training, the Canny Collar® is not the best tool of choice because she could get out of it with her many different body movements. It does not latch at the bottom but works quite similar to the bridle reins. If you plan on using a head collar to do a lot of movement (other than leash walking). I would not recommend this tool as it must be held taut to maintain its position on the dog's face. This tool is the best choice if you plan on doing a lot of walking. I have used these on a camping trip because they clasp around a dog's neck, but while they are not in use, they were available and convenient just in case I needed to use them.

All photos of Boy and Canny Collar® by Bryan Huntting
Michelle is holding the Canny Collar® flat. This part will fit like a regular collar.

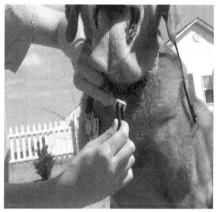

Once the collar is in place, Michelle is pulling the strap through the yellow plastic.

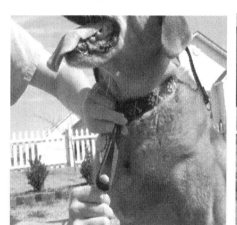

Once the strap is pulled, Michelle places the strap over Boy's mouth.

Once the strap is over Boy's nose, Michelle clasps the two straps behind boy's head with leash.

A **Snoot Loop®** is another option for a head halter. The Snoot Loop® adjusts with buckles from the sides of dog's mouth unlike all the other head halters. This head halter will fit breeds that have a different shaped face such as a bulldog.

Photo from Snoot Loop®

Holt® (pictured below) is my new favorite for head halters. Currently this is the collar that Boy and I use when we do therapy visits. The Holt® fits similar to the Holti®, but it adjusts on the bottom like the Gentle Leader®. There is a big confusion with brand names here. I am not recommending the Holti® (with the "I") because, from my experience, it always moves up into the dog's eyes causing discomfort.

Photo by author

166

Where to purchase these tools?

Most pet food stores carry the Gentle Leader® and Holt®, or you can find them on www.amazon.com.

Other websites include the following:
Canny Collar® www.cannyco.us
Snoot Loop® www.snootloop.com

As a a huge supporter of local shops, I always encourage you to check with them first to help out our small business owners.

Michelle's Protocol for Head Halter Desensitization

Purpose: This is a head halter desensitization protocol with the purpose of using positive training to help a canine have a positive, comfortable, and relaxed response to the head halter, and to encourage him to freely and willingly allow the head halter to be put on.

The following protocol is designed to be used in short sessions and without progression to the next step until the dog is showing a happy, relaxed response to the current exercise.

How long should I conduct a session? This answer depends on the dog, but the general rule is 3-5 minutes. If you have an older dog that has been clicker trained, there is a good chance that you will be able to train for a longer period of time. I would not, however, work longer than 15 minutes. Adjusting to the head halter is not an easy process for any dog, and we always want to end a training session with the dog wanting more.

How can I tell if my dog is uncomfortable? With this protocol the goal is to keep him comfortable and associate the head halter as a good thing. One of the signs that he is uncomfortable is if he were to back up. If this happens then simply slow down the process and go back to the last step that he was comfortable. Be sure to keep the sessions short as well. Do not push your dog too far too fast.

What you will need: clicker, treats, and head halter

Head Halter Desensitization Protocol
- Present head halter to your dog and give him treats.
- Place head halter behind your back.
- Repeat several times until you see the dog is happy to see the head halter and anticipating the treats.
- Place head halter on the floor and when the dog moves toward the head halter, click, and treat.
- Continue to repeat until the dog is consistently touching it. (You can leave the head halter out on the floor, but if you see that he is not completely relaxed with it in sight, then after he touches it, treat, and then place the head halter behind your back. Continue this process until you see a relaxed response.)
- Once you have a consistent response, start delaying the click to work toward a longer nose hold (or longer touch) on the head halter.
- Repeat until your dog has a consistent longer nose hold.
- Once you have a consistent nose hold, hold the head halter with the entrance toward him. (You will need to hold the halter open with your hand. I would suggest using your dominant hand with your fingers spread wide to keep it open).
- Click any time the dog starts putting his nose toward or in the entrance area.
- If canine holds his nose in all the way, give a jackpot. (As a reminder, a jackpot is a handful of treats delivered one treat at a time but quickly). You can bait the dog at this time by holding a treat on the other side of the head halter. Once the dog is consistently putting his nose into the head halter, start clicking the longer he holds with his nose in the head halter.
- As he puts his nose into the head halter, move the straps up and down; click and treat.
- Once your dog has a relaxed response, start moving straps up around his ears; click and treat.
- Repeat until he's relaxed.

No clicker needed for remaining steps:
- With the head halter straps loose, quickly latch and unlatch, and deliver a treat. Continue doing this until you see a relaxed response.
- Tighten the straps, introduce the head halter, quickly latch and unlatch, and deliver treat.

- Place the head halter on, latch and delay a few seconds, unlatch, and deliver treat.
- Continue the process of latching/unlatching, and treat as you lengthen time.
- Be sure to vary the time by keeping the leash attached for 2 seconds, 5 seconds, 3 seconds, 1 second. Continue this process until you have attained a comfortable 30 seconds.
- Do 5 separate sessions of 30 seconds at a time, rewarding throughout.

Leash
- Clip leash on/off head halter. Be sure to treat during this process.
- Allow the leash to hang for 5 seconds while treating.
- Clip leash on/off head halter. Be sure to treat during this process.
- Allow the leash to hang 10 seconds while treating, unclip leash, allow leash to hang 3 seconds, unclip leash; leash on 20 seconds, unclip leash; leash on 10 seconds, unclip leash; leash on 40 seconds, unclip. Continue varying the process until you've worked until one minute. Be sure not to act excited when the leash is unclipped. You want to use your happy rewarding voice while the leash is on the dog.

Walking with Head Halter
- Encourage the dog's head to stay up so he doesn't have the opportunity to rub against the ground or try to pull the head halter off. Be sure to hold the leash in toward you so there is one foot of length between you and your dog and you are ready to pull up if needed. Every time your dog looks at you during this process, click, praise, and treat.
- Start walking your dog around the house, the driveway, and the yard for short sessions. Clickable behaviors include appropriate walking beside you or looking up at you.
- Gradually continue to increase walk time with the head halter on. Be sure to deliver lots of treats and praise during this time.

Harnesses

No-pull Harnesses have worked for a handful of my clients. This harness is designed to have the leash hook in the front, and when the dog pulls, it turns him back toward you. Walk Your Dog with Love® is a harness my colleagues recommend for a no pull harness. This particular harness doesn't chafe like other brands (www.walkyourdogwithlove.com).

Photo by author

A Regular Harness has worked for me with success. (Many companies make these, but Kong® brand is one of my favorites.) Some dogs pull because they feel pressure around their neck. For these dogs putting them in a harness is very helpful. I really encourage puppy owners as well as petite breed owners to use a regular harness. There are a lot of fancy harnesses that claim to do great things, but I enjoy the one that is pictured on opposite page. It's important that your dog is comfortable. Years ago I found one that was padded on the chest with sheep's wool that my dog seemed to enjoy. Please do not get a harness that is designed to make corrections! These special designs prove counterproductive to your training as you want to make positive associations with the leash. Also, if you have a puppy or a new dog and he is learning a new behavior, how can you correct him for something he doesn't know? This type of training leads to confusion and frustration in the dogs. The sole purpose of using the harness is to eliminate any pressure on the neck.

In addition, the notion that you will have less control with a harness on a large dog is not true. Considering the size of a large, untrained dog, I wouldn't likely choose a harness, but it is simply untrue that a harness should never be used on a large dog.

Let me tell you, folks, Boy is 80 pounds and walks beautifully with a harness. Why? Because I taught him exactly what I wanted. In fact, from his behavior I can actually see that he enjoys being on a harness. Granted, we don't use the harness all the time. There are times when Boy is on his Canny Collar® (especially when his sisters are walking with us) and other times he is on a Holt® when we are doing therapy work and moving around more. There is a time and a place for every tool.

Photo by Bryan Huntting

Boy has already stepped into the harness, and Michelle is clasping the harness on the side clip.

Photo by Bryan Huntting

A regular harness has clips on the dog's back for the leash.

The last tool

I debated on sharing my last tool because I very rarely ever recommend this tool. Over the many years of training, I have recommended this tool less than five times and only for very specific cases. One occasion was for a retired veteran who had numerous seizures daily. He couldn't easily maintain balance so he walked with a cane. We had tried all the other tools, and the dog was still out of control. However, with the Starmark® collar, he was able to walk her with more ease and maintain his balance. For this particular case, it was a matter of safety for my client and also a matter of quality of life for the dog.

I included it here only because the purpose of my book is to set you up for success with your dog so that you can work toward enjoying each other.

The Starmark® Collar

The Starmark® Collar is flat on the outside like a regular collar, but the inside is similar to a prong collar. It is made of hard plastic, and the links may be taken out or added depending on the size of your dog. When correctly fitting this collar, you should not allow the collar to be fitted to hang loose around the dog's neck. This collar is designed to be snug (but not digging) to the neck. For safety reasons, it is also important that this collar is taken off when you are not training.

Let's just start with who this collar is NOT for and how it should NOT be used. It should not be used for puppies or for petite breeds, and it should also not be used as a hard correction.

Honestly, I have found I have *more* control with the head halters than with the Starmark®. For me, I would much rather walk a Great Dane with a Holt® than with the Starmark® simply because I have more control over a dog from his head than his neck. There are just a few, rare cases where I have exhausted one hundred percent of all other tools, and the Starmark® is my last, or best option due to physical limitations. For me, the quality of life is important. If a pet owner has truly tried all the other tools and none are helping them to walk their dog, then I would rather they try this tool to see if they are able to successfully walk their dog versus their dog being stuck indoors for the rest of his life or, perhaps worse yet, relinquished to a shelter because he can't be controlled.

When you are training with this collar, be sure you do not keep a constant tightness on the leash. Try to maintain a "J" shape. This is vital because a constant tight pressure on the leash will potentially hurt your dog.

Summary of Using Tools
It's vital that all of your tools are fitted properly and used correctly. If fitted incorrectly, the collar can potentially cause harm to your dog or the dog, could possibly get loose from you. Almost all of the tools come with demo DVDs that will coach you through the fitting process. If you are ever in doubt, you can talk to a trainer or sales clerk who has specific knowledge of the product. Many times the representative of that product has visited the store and trained them how to fit correctly.

No matter what tool you use, do not allow your dog to pull. Even if you have a Canny® or a Gentle Leader®, you may be tempted to allow your dog to apply pressure, which is counterproductive, during the walk. *If there is any tension on the leash, evaluate why and adjust the situation. We don't want to undo all the hard work that you've been doing!*

If you have ever played sports, you know that practice doesn't always make perfect. It does, however, make permanent. In other words, if you are practicing your sport every day with a bad form, your performance will suffer, so make sure your form is always good with leash walking, tool or no tool.

CHAPTER 12

MULTIPLE DOGS

Photo by Miranda Vallade

I once heard the quote that dogs are like chips; you just can't have just one. It's true. Less than six months out of college, I had three puppies. I am happy with my "pack" who are all with me still. They are a wonderful pack. We are beautiful together.

One of the things that we learned to do together was walk as a team. They have traveled all over the United States with me. We have lived in a townhome, an acreage in Iowa, a condo in Orlando, and now our home in North Carolina. We had to learn to work together and make the most of our situations. I must say, Orlando was pretty difficult with the abundance of ducks and lizards. I would be peacefully walking along, and before I realized it, my dogs had spotted a lizard. Before I made the adjustment on the leash, they had pulled my arm nearly out of the socket. However, we worked through all the challenges and were successful, even with the ducks, by the time we left Orlando.

Walking multiple dogs is certainly quite different from walking one dog. There are many things to consider and train when walking multiple dogs, such as getting them used to walking next to each other, learning how to position the dogs, and helping the dogs maintain focus. Focus is crucial because often times the dogs feed off of each other's excitement.

Where to Start
If you have multiple dogs, each dog must first be trained individually. I didn't take all three of my dogs out together when they were going through their eight-week basic courses. They were received individual time with me during the foundational training time. If you have multiple dogs, begin training each of them individually for eight weeks using the impulse control, focus, and other leash walking techniques. If you want a well-built home, you don't want to start with a weak foundation. The same is true with leash walking. You want to make sure that the foundation is strong and doesn't have any weak points before attempting to walk multiple dogs together. Take the time now with each individual dog to invest in the foundational time.

All the leash walking skills taught in this book will help you gain polite leash walking.

When You Start Adding Together
A rule when training: when you raise one criterion, you lower another. For example, if you were working on *stay* with your dog you will start with standing close to him and work on getting a longer stay, like 15 seconds. This is what trainers call duration. Once you've established duration, then you will add distance, standing a few steps away from your dog. When we start working on distance, this is considered "raising a criterion." When you raise a criterion, you want to lower your previous one. In other words, when you start adding distance, in this specific example, you will not expect a 15 second stay in addition to the distance. You will lower the expectation to a 5-second stay while adding distance, for example.

As I said, when you are training multiple dogs, you want to work with them individually as working with two or more dogs is too distracting when they are learning new behaviors. Once the foundation has been built individually with each dog, we will then add a second dog. When you start working with the two dogs, don't expect the same level of focus and impulse control that you would have individually. You will need to work with both dogs until you reach the desired level of focus and impulse control.

Once you have the desired focus walking two, you are ready to add a third dog. You will then alternate walking the dogs together when adding the new dog. Using my dogs as an example:

I work with all three dogs in sets of two until I got the desired level of focus. Morgan and Belle are now focused as they walk together. Now I walk Boy and Morgan together until they are focused. Now I alternate and walk Belle and Boy together. Once I get the desired level of focus with two at a time, I will add all three together and work with them to the desired level of focus.

Belle & Morgan → Focused→   Belle & Boy→ Focused →
Morgan & Boy→ Focused →   Boy, Morgan & Belle→ Focused

Safety is important as well. When I walk all three of my (large) dogs together I always use a tool which I don't normally use when walking them individually. Because three large breed dogs have more muscle power than I, I use precaution and have them on head halters when I walk all three simultaneously. I feel it's safer for me with these tools *just in case* moments arise. The head halters give me more confidence so the walk goes much better overall. Obviously, if you have small to medium breeds, head halters may not be your tool of choice. It all depends on the comfort level of each handler.

How to Hold the Leash
In the chapter on leash handling skills, I talk specifically about how to use the leash to communicate to dogs. However, there are other considerations when learning how the leashes are held when walking multiple dogs. I prefer to hold each leash separately (2 leashes in my right hand and one leash in my left hand) as we are walking with each dog positioned at different leash lengths. I make movements and slight pressure and release of slight pressure to constantly communicate to my dogs with adjustments of the leash. There isn't a "right" or "wrong" way to holding the leashes, but I think there are certainly more effective ways of holding them. Bottom line, it is the preference of the individual handler. I tell all my students to try different positions with the leash to see how it feels. I

have learned many things just by trying. The most important thing is that you and your dog are both enjoying each other and enjoying the quality of life with your dog.

When I walk all three of my dogs together, I keep them close to my body. I do not allow them to sniff when we all walk together unless I release them to *go sniff* and potty. Keeping them close helps to reinforce working together as a team. We all enjoy walking more when we work together.

Photo by Miranda Vallade

In these photos, please note how I communicate different things through each hand. For Belle (on my left) I am holding back on the leash because with the turn she is essentially pivoting around versus moving around as Boy and Morgan.

Photo by Miranda Vallade

Photo by Miranda Vallade

Notice how I am holding back on the leash for Belle (on the left) and I am also using my body to move into her with my left leg and using the bend of my right leg to encourage the turn from Morgan and Boy. I am relaxed on Morgan's and Boy's leashes as they need to continue moving forward for the turn.

The Release

In the chapter on Reinforcement (7), I talk about a *go to* release, so if you observe that your dog wants to sniff a specific blade of grass, you will cue "go sniff," and release him. When I am out with all three of my dogs and I want them to sniff and go potty, I will release them with "okay, go potty." My release word is consistent as I always precede with the word "okay." Whatever word you decide to use as the, *it's okay to disengage cue,* be consistent. I also follow the release cue with what I would like them to do. In this particular case I told them to "go potty."

Photo by Miranda Vallade

Photo by Miranda Vallade

Pick A Side

As I have walked my dogs, I have noticed just from observation that they prefer different positions or to be close to a specific dog. As you are working with your dogs, observe their behavior. If Belle is more comfortable walking beside Morgan, then why not allow her to do so? Position them so they are comfortable and you are comfortable as well. Close observation of your dogs will help you know how to position each one.

Training Exercises for Multiple Dog Homes

After the leash walking foundation is built with each individual dog, there are exercises that you can do with both (or all) of them together.

Stand Stay:

I learned *stand stay* in my obedience class. My trainer Pat told us that our vet would love us if our dogs could *stand stay* while being weighed and during the examination. I do use *stand stay* for vet visits, but I also use the *stand stay* on almost every walk. I find the cue helpful if I need to stop and tie my shoe, before I cross the street or make an abrupt stop. A *sit stay* takes more time because the leashes have to be readjusted, and it's faster for them to move forward from a standing position than from a sitting position.

When you start teaching the *stand stay*, it is important to train each individual dog first and then train with two dogs or more together just as I explained earlier in this chapter.

How to Teach:

Stand is an important cue. You can cue a *stand* and *stay* while you are on a walk, for a vet exam, during grooming, and so much more.

Here's how it's done:

Lure your dog into a sit by, placing a lure (treat) in front of his nose and moving it straight out. This movement will encourage a stand posture. When he stands, mark (click) and reward; say "stand", and reward with a treat. Do 4-5 repetitions and end the session.

Later in the week, fade the treat and use your hand (no treat) to encourage a *stand*. You will hold your hand as if holding a treat in front of your dog's nose and move it straight out. Again, this movement will encourage a *stand* posture, just as with the treat. When he stands, mark (click), say, "Stand", and reward with treat. Do 4-5 repetitions and end the session.

"Dogs" as a cue:
Instead of saying my dogs' individual names, I use a cue that means *Hello everyone! I need you all to pay attention to me!* When I want everyone to do something, I will address the group as "dogs." So, for example, when I want all the dogs to come inside, I will cue, "Dogs, come!" If I want an individual dog to respond, I will use a name as in, "Belle, sit." If I need the entire group to stand, I will say, "Dogs, stand stay." A group cue is helpful and allows them to understand clearly the difference.

How to Train
To begin training a group cue, I would start with *sit*. When first teaching this group cue, start in a small area, like a room. As the group of dogs is with you, cue, "Dogs, sit." Say, "Good" to each individual dog after he sits, and once everyone is in a seated position, treat.

Watch:
You can do the watch training exercise that is described on page 203 to help them focus as a group. Position all three of them in the sitting position, and say, "Watch," and treat them individually once you gain eye contact from all of them.

Photo by Cheryl Kenyon

Trouble Shooting:

If your dogs tend to feed off of each other's excitement when walking together, then I would highly recommend using the Michelle's Protocol for Focus & Relaxation with all of the dogs together (page 215). Of course, you would begin with the protocol with each dog individually. I would start the protocol in the house for the full 14 days, and once you've successfully completed the sequence, then do the entire protocol with all of your dogs in the back-yard and then the front-yard. This routine will help them learn to work together as well as maintain those skills when they are all together. When I am conducting the protocol outdoors, I modify it a bit as it is obliviously intended as an indoor activity. Don't worry what the neighbors think! I know mine probably think I am crazy as I am dancing around in my front yard with dogs that are enrolled in my board and train program. As long as dogs leave my program focused, calm, and exercising impulse control, I am a happy camper. Just wait until I start yodeling! If dogs could only talk, they would probably talk to each other about the crazy dancing trainer.

When walking multiple dogs, you may experience "redirected aggression" (when one dog can't get to something and takes it out on the other dog). If this happens, contact a professional in your area. Please see chapter 15 as to how to find a great trainer or animal behaviorist. This book is not written with the intention of focusing on aggression or reactive issues other than an overly excited dog. If you have such a serious issues, be sure to contact a qualified professional right away, but in the mean-time, do not walk the dogs together, though continue to walk them individually.

Training More Than One Dog

You can set your multiple dogs up for success by training them individually and then working with them together by always being fair when raising criteria and then taking time to train them as a group.

CHAPTER 13

PETITE & SHORT BREEDS

Photo by Bryan Huntting

I love petite breeds. Training them is so different from large breeds that I felt it was worth mentioning some tips and techniques. These breeds face different challenges and have different issues that require adjustment to the training regimen. I trained for a couple who had a medium-sized dog but now have several Chihuahuas. They also remark about how different the process was for them.

No matter how small and adorable your dog is, I encourage you to *allow your dog to make decisions of where to move on his own.* What exactly do I mean by this? I have noticed when training families with petite breeds, that when I say, for example, "Go ahead and encourage your dog down from the couch," the owner will walk over, pick the dog up, and place him on the floor. If the dog is a Lab or even a Great Dane, this action would not be an option. We would have to use our body movement or a sound to encourage the dog off the coach. Owners of petite breeds need to become aware that it is important that their dogs are learning to make good decisions on their own. This can only happen if you allow your dog to make these decisions when positioning your petite breed or when teaching leash walking.

Just like with puppies, small sessions may be required depending on the breed of small dog that you own. When I was young, I had a friend who was significantly shorter than I. When we would go out to play, I would be striding normally, and often times she would gasp and say, *"Oh man, Michelle! I walk two to three steps to your one!"* She was having a hard time keeping up with me even though I was using my normal stride. Remember that petite breeds walk several steps to your one, so shorter training sessions may be required. However, this may not be true for all breeds. Just be sure to observe your dog and set him up for success by adjusting the sessions and pace to accommodate his size and needs.

Treats are also another important consideration when training a petite breed. I wouldn't be worried about giving half of a cup of cooked meat to a Lab during the process of training, but this amount would constitute a Thanksgiving feast to a petite breed. One of the things that I recommend for petite breeds is using a lick as a treat. Earlier in the book (Chapter 2) I referenced the Lickety Stik®. You can also use a stuffed Kong® with peanut butter and allow your dog to lick once or twice during the process of training. Another option would be a jar (or a bag) of baby food.

Photo by author

Getting used to the Harness

Many petite breeds shut down after they put a harness on. It's important to get them used to a harness because we never walk a petite breed on a leash connected to their collar because their necks are so delicate.

Still, your petite breeds must be leashed when taking them out in public. Owners risk their very small dog escaping to run off leash in the neighborhood. A petite breed is not likely to be spotted by a car, so please be sure to work on making the harness a delightful object in your dog's eyes, and always take your dog out of the house on leash.

Harness Desensitization Protocol
Please note that every harness will differ, so adjust the protocol as needed, using it as a guide.

What you will need: clicker, treats, and harness.

- Present the harness to the dog and give treats.
- Place the harness behind your back.
- Repeat several times until you see the dog happy to see the harness and anticipating the treats.
- Place the harness on the floor and when the dog moves toward the harness, click and treat.
- Continue to repeat until the dog is consistently touching the harness. (You can leave the harness out on the floor, but if you see that he is not completely relaxed when it is in sight, once he touches it, treat, then place the harness behind your back. Continue this until you see a relaxed response.)
- Once you have a consistent response, start delaying the click to work toward a longer nose hold on the harness.
- Repeat until the dog has a consistent longer nose hold.
- Once you have a consistent nose hold, place the harness with the entrance facing the dog. (You will need to hold the harness open with your hands.)
- Click anytime the dog starts putting his nose toward or in the entrance area.
- If the dog holds his nose in all the way, give a jackpot. (Again, a jackpot is a handful of treats delivered one treat at a time) You can bait the dog at this time by holding a treat on the other side of the harness. Once the dog is consistently putting his nose into the harness, start clicking the longer holds with his nose in the harness.
- As the dog puts his nose in the harness, click and treat.
- Once the dog has a relaxed response, allow the harness to freely lie around his neck; click and treat.
- Repeat until he's relaxed.

No clicker needed for remaining steps:
- With the harness still loosely placed around the dog's neck, lift his right paw and let go; treat.

- Repeat until he's relaxed.
- With the harness still loosely placed around the dog's neck, lift his right paw and place into harness, (treat).
- Repeat until he's relaxed.
- With the harness straps loose and his right leg through harness, latch and unlatch the harness and deliver a treat. Continue doing this until you see a relaxed response.
- Tighten the straps, introduce harness, latch and unlatch, and deliver a treat.
- Place harness on, latch and delay a few seconds, unlatch, and deliver a treat.
- Continue the process of latching/unlatching and treat as you lengthen time.
- Be sure to vary the time by doing a short unlatch/latch for 2 seconds, 5 seconds, 3 seconds, 1 second. Continue this process until you have attained a comfortable 30 seconds.
- Do 5 separate sessions of 30 seconds at a time, rewarding throughout.

Leash
- Clip leash on/off harness. Be sure to treat during this process.
- Allow the leash to hang for 5 seconds while treating.
- Clip leash on/off harness. Be sure to treat during this process.
- Allow the leash to hang 10 seconds while treating, unclip leash, allow leash to hang 3 seconds; unclip leash; leash on 20 seconds; unclip leash; leash on 10 seconds; unclip leash; leash on 40 seconds; unclip. Continue varying the process until you've worked for one minute. Don't act excited when the leash is unclipped. You want the happy, rewarding voice while the leash is on the dog.

Walking with a Leashed Harness
- Every time your dog looks at you during this process, click, praise, and treat.
- Start walking your dog around the house, the driveway, and the yard for short sessions. Clickable behaviors are relaxed walking beside you or looking up at you.

- Continue to gradually increase the walk time with the harness on. Be sure to deliver lots of treats and praise during this time.

Building Confidence

I have found that allowing the petite breed dogs to choose to move on their own helps build confidence. I also would highly recommend Michelle's Protocol for Focus & Relaxation that is in the Resource Chapter 16.

As you are out in the community, please keep your dog's comfort in mind. People automatically see your tiny dog and think he is so adorable that they just can't help themselves, and they go crazy wanting to pet and cuddle your adorable little puppy even though you may have a seven-year old Chihuahua that only looks like a puppy. It's important to read your dog's body language, and if you know he will be uncomfortable in a certain situation, then don't allow him to enter the situation. Under such circumstances, you have the option of making the situation look different to the dog or simply leave the situation entirely. Be your dog's advocate. Building a trusting relationship will help with building your dog's confidence.

Hide the Treat

One of the major issues with petite breeds is confidence building. I talked about the importance of allowing them to choose to move on their own in "Michelle's Protocol for Focus & Relaxation," and now I am going to share with you a nose game that will help build confidence.

I actually played "Hide the Treat" game with my dogs in my parents barn out of boredom and a desire to do more training with them. I placed a treat on top of their dog door before I left them for the night. The next day the treat was gone, so I thought to myself "this might be fun." I told all of my dogs to "sit stay" on the other side of the room so they could see where I was hiding the treats. Then, I released them and said "go find!" They scrambled to find all of the treats I had hidden in very easy places with one always placed on top of the dog door.

I gradually increased the difficulty, hiding the treats in less obvious places as they watched me. They were having a blast and quickly caught on.

Eventually while the dogs were in a "sit stay," I hid all the treats outside of the room in places the dogs couldn't see. I now play this game in my living room. I love watching them sniffing down the entire couch and pushing their nose way under pillows. They have a blast!

Heel on the Bleachers

I don't know how tall you are, but I am 5' 10," and working with petite breeds is back breaking. They may not be able to pull you all over the place as a larger breed can, but they can surely kink your back from all that bending over they require of their handlers. So instead of working harder, let's work smarter. We are going to find a set of bleachers that we can use to help us as we work on "heel." There are a variety of training exercises that can be conducted using the bleachers.

Target Stick: For this exercise you will need your target stick, leash, treats, and bait bag. Place your dog on the lowest row of bleachers and work on *touch* every two steps.

Eye Target: For this exercise you will need a clicker, leash, treats, and bait bag. Place your dog on the lowest row of bleachers, and as you are walking, mark any eye contact from your dog.

Note: As a matter of safety, it is important that your dog is on a harness and that you walk very close to your dog. Come in on the leash (shorten it) as Jennifer demonstrates in the photos opposite. It's important when using the bleachers that your dog is comfortable and has a good experience.

Photos taken by Miranda Vallade
Jennifer has Gertie leashed on the harness.

Teaching Heel with a Target Stick

I still believe that you are able to use the leash as a means of communication with your small dog just as you would with any breed. However, because of the delicate state of a petite breed's neck, I would not want to encourage any students of mine to use leash manipulation for the *heel* exercise. If you have a breed like a Bulldog, Rat Terrier, or a breed that is sturdy but short, using the leash manipulation described in the Heel Chapter (10) is acceptable. For the petite breeds that have a delicate neck, I recommend a hands-off technique and training with a target stick. They need to be on a harness for this exercise.

I would highly recommend making your own target stick by using a wooden dowel with a soft ping pong ball at the end. The ball is a great target. Before you use the target stick for heel, you need to start with the very beginning steps of teaching the target stick, which is described in Chapter 6. Your dog will need to know how to successfully follow the stick left, right, up, and down to begin using the target stick for heel. When using the target stick, the handler must pay attention to the way his body is used to communicate.

Photos taken by Miranda Vallade

Please note the body language in the photos. Jennifer (left) was having a difficult time getting Gertie to move and follow the target stick. Notice the difference in the body postures of the two handlers. One encouraged no movement while the other elicited much movement. Michelle's knees (right) are bent slightly, and her posture is bent and moving forward slightly as she presents the target stick. (Some people think I really have a way with dogs because they instantly follow me, but it's not magic; it's body language. If you aren't successful in eliciting movement from your dog, then check-in with your own body language and movement. Dogs respond to the most subtle things.)

In the photo on the left, notice the difference of Gertie's movement based on the way Jennifer is moving her body.

Photo by Miranda Vallade

192

Step One: Start by positioning your dog at your left side. You will want to treat and praise this position. Work on this positioning for two days, two to three sessions per day. Use your target stick to position your dog. Start your dog out in front of you and move the target stick around (almost behind you) and then back to your left side and then up to encourage a sit.

Remaining Photos in this chapter by Miranda Vallade

Gertie decided that she would rather target the stick with her eyes than her nose. This was a first for Michelle, but she adjusted her target stick accordingly because what she was doing was working. This is why the target stick is positioned higher than it traditionally would be if a canine were targeting with his nose.

The above diagram demonstrates the movement of the target sick. Starting with the dog in front of the handler, the handler will move the target stick, arcing around, moving almost behind the body, and then up to encourage a sit.

Step 2: Reinforcing   Step 3: Are you ready?   Start with left foot

Step Two: Once your dog has learned how to quickly move into the heel starting position, then strongly reinforce the sitting position at your left side.

Step Three: Now that your dog understands how to get into a heel position and he is sitting on your left side, you will ask, "Are you ready?"

If you have eye contact, step with your left leg and while you are moving your *left leg** out, you will show your target stick at the same time. Take two to three steps, and before you stop, cue a sit or use your target stick to move him into a sit.

*Starting with your left foot is a non-verbal indicator to your dog that you will be working in the heel position. There are times I have forgotten to say "heel," but was thinking it, and out of habit, stepped out with my left foot. I realized five minutes later that my dogs were heeling, though I had never verbally cued it. Always starting with your left foot is a good habit to get into.

You will continue working toward increasing the number of steps and follow through with the turns and using the target stick. (Demonstrated in Chapter 10)

Let's Go

As described in the Chapter 8, the *let's go* cue should be done in the same manner as for larger breed dogs. It is VERY important that your petite breed or short breed dog is on a harness for this exercise to protect against possible injury.

Steps with Let's Go

1) Start walking.
2) If your dog goes out in front of you, stop and make a sound.
3) Start backing up until your dog is behind you or at your side.
4) When he's behind or beside you, click and quickly move forward again.
5) During this entire process anytime your dog walks two or more steps alongside you, click (or mark), and deliver a treat. Verbally give your dog feedback as well.

Step 3: Back up until your dog is alongside or behind you; click

Step 4: When your dog is alongside you quickly move forward.

Control on leash

Follow the Leader

Doing the "Follow the Leader" exercise is good for the petite breeds as well as puppies. I go into detail about this exercise on page 202. It's important to use your body language when doing this exercise. Please note Jennifer's body language of bending forward slightly, moving in the direction that she wants her dog to move as well as occasionally tapping her leg with her hand. She is also using sounds to encourage Gertie to follow her.

Petite Breeds

Training leash walking to smaller breeds is no more or less difficult than training large breed dogs, but it does present a bit of a different spin on the procedure as you learn to adapt the steps to the smaller size of your pet. Still, it can be just as much fun to train a Chihuahua as it is to train a Great Dane.

CHAPTER 14

NEW TO THE LEASH

What an opportunity you have if you are starting a new puppy with these techniques! You are able to start off with no bad habits to break! I had two beautiful Great Pyrenees puppies join Miss Belle's Etiquette Boarding School™. Both puppies were farm dogs and had never really been taken for a walk on a leash before. Because the owner hadn't introduced any bad habits, learning polite leash walking came very easy for them. For example, if puppies get used to the feeling of pressure on their throat, they will always adjust to that feeling. Therefore, I encourage puppy owners to use a harness to ensure there is no pressure on the reflex muscle..

The leash must be an especially positive experience since it's new to the puppy. Please be aware of your dog's body language as discussed in earlier chapters. "Listen" to your dog. If he is showing signs of stress or discomfort, then slow down or make the exercise look different to him. This change could be something as simple as dropping a leash. The exercises in this chapter will work well with a new rescue dog as well as puppies.

Note: I find with puppies or shorter breeds that a six-foot leash is much more comfortable for me than the typical four-foot leash.

Leash Exercises
For young puppies or a rescue that has never gotten use to a collar, it get them used to the collar before even starting with the leash.

Collar Exercise

It will take the puppy some time to get used to the collar and the leash. Be aware of the puppy's level of comfort during the process of getting him familiar with these tools, so be sure to watch for displacement behavior, and to go slow and take a lot of breaks.

Collar: Have treats readily available. Collar exercises are ones that I typically don't use a clicker for as the clicker is loud and will potentially be close to your puppy's ear.

Collar Exercises:

Move the collar around, then treat.
Grab the collar with one hand, then treat.
Grab the collar from the left side, then treat.
Grab the collar from the right side, then treat.
Grab the collar from underneath the chin, then treat.
Take the collar off and put it back on, then treat.
Grab the collar from on top of the neck, then treat.
Grab collar with two hands, then treat.

Next Step: Do all the exercises while sitting on the ground next to the puppy. Once your puppy is happy with these exercises and is showing no signs of stress, stand up and do all of the following exercises listed above. This position will help him learn that it's a good thing when you reach out towards him.

Note: Sometimes it helps to deliver a treat while simultaneously moving the collar around.

Introduction to Leash

When acclimating a puppy to a leash, I (usually, but not required) use a leash with no handle. I allow the puppy to roam around, allowing the leash to drag so that he gets used to the feel of it. It's extremely important that the owner is observing and actively involved during this process. We don't want any negative associations like getting the leash caught on something. I would recommend doing this activity for only a few moments once a day for a couple of weeks.

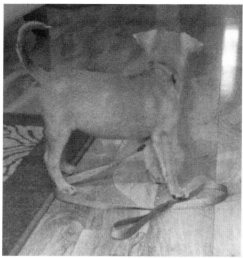

Photo by author

During the time that you allow puppy to drag the leash, you can encourage puppy to follow you by making kissy sounds and patting your leg. Be sure to make this a very positive experience with lots of praise and treats.

Next Step: After two weeks you can occasionally begin to pick up the leash for a few seconds as the puppy is following and drop it again. You can do this activity indoors as well as in your backyard.

Note: For older rescues I will assume that they have been on a leash at some point in their life so this step may not be necessary. However, I would recommend doing the collar exercise. Please be aware of dog's body language during the collar exercise as some older dogs can be very touchy. Go slow and pay attention to what they are saying.

Tethering

I am a huge fan of tether training. Tethering helps with so many things including potty training, relationship building, check ins (the puppy or dog keeping an eye on you with a look in your direction), communication, focus, and polite leash walking skills. If you can do this training 30 minutes or more a day, that would be great. When I did this with my own rescue dog, I used a carabineer (metal loop with closure pictured on next page) attached to the leash and tied around my belt loop.

Photo by author

(a) Picture of carabineer above. (b) Kristen demonstrates how to use a leash with a belt loop without a carabineer.

As an option to using a carabineer, you can loop the leash through the handle and attach to your dog (pictured above).

I recommend tethering for your puppy during the potty training days. For other dogs I would try to tether from two to four weeks while you are really focusing on your leash walking skills. If you are able, keep your dog tethered while you are dusting and doing things around the house, even while you are watching TV because you will generally get up to get something to drink or a refill of popcorn. I think that you will both learn a lot about each other during this process.

Note: Your dog should have plenty of slack in the leash. The leash that was used for these demo pictures was only a four-foot leash and I would normally recommend a six-foot leash, for a long-term exercise. Be sure to prevent any negative experience. Having the tether too tight can be extremely uncomfortable and also give potential to unnecessary pressure.

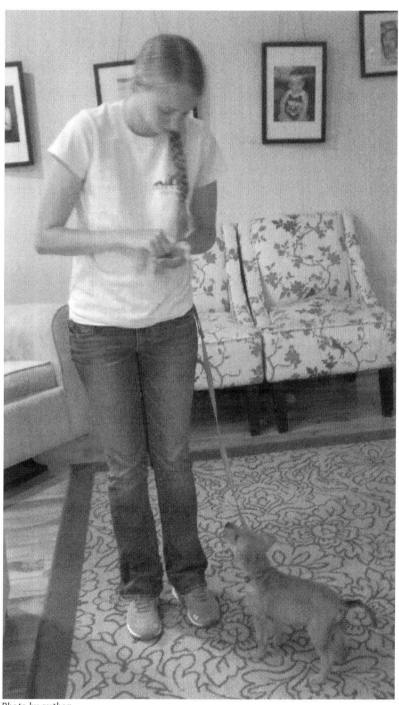

Photo by author

Follow the Leader

I love training with the leash dragging and picking it up on and off while training with puppies. As I mentioned, avoid negative experiences, so please be sure that whatever environment you are working in is free of debris or anything that the leash could potentially snag on. A clear environment is especially important for the "follow the leader" game.

With the "Follow the Leader" game, you will want to take a handful of treats and have your running shoes on in your yard. This game can be played in the front or backyard with your leash dragging. I want you to make this a fun game where you jog a little bit with an excited voice as you are moving around the yard patting your left leg. As soon as puppy follows you or aligns himself with your leg, praise and deliver treats and continue the game. I would not recommend petting as a reward during this time. Continue with the game three more times. Be sure not to go too long as we don't want the puppy to get tired and lose interest, and we also don't want to work him to the point where he can't bring himself back down, emotionally speaking. Have lots of fun with this game; make it fun for you and puppy (pictured on page 196).

During Tether Training

As you are working with your puppy, be watchful for looks from your puppy at which time you can praise and treat. We want to encourage as much eye contact as possible. Remember that it is not natural for dogs to make direct eye contact. In fact, in their world, eye contact is perceived as threatening. So you can encourage them in other exercises to make direct eye contact, but during tether training, I would like you to reward for a general look at your face. I have noticed dogs checking in with their peripheral vision as we are walking, but I think for the sake of this exercise, reward them when they look directly at your facial area.

Photo by author

Photo by Amber Craig

Check Ins

Anytime you are with your dog and you notice him look at you, praise and treat, a behavior we call "check ins." Check ins are extremely important in *all* training programs, but they are truly the foundation of leash walking. Remember you are with your dance partner and communication is key. The eye contact is a foundation for that level of communication.

Watch Exercise

When I lived in Orlando for six months, I dedicated much of my time to training my dogs. Once a day I took a handful of treats and went outside of our condo and did this *watch* exercise every day for two weeks. It was during this time that I saw improvements in our leash walking skills, and I believe that it will do the same for yours.

- Take a handful of treats and head to your front porch.
- Keep the handful of treats in your dominant hand.
- Take one treat in your dominant hand, and place it in front of your dog's nose.
- Almost as soon as you place it in front of your dog's nose, start drawing it up to your face to the side of your eye.

- As you are drawing it up to your face, say, "W-a-t-c-h."
- Deliver the treat as long as his eyes are looking at your face.

Photo by author

It is during this exercise that you can encourage your dog to look directly in the eyes. (Remember, if you have multiple dogs, do this exercise individually and then add together.)

Photos by author

Lots of Breaks
Whether you have a puppy or a new rescue, it is very important to take a lot of breaks during the training process. I was amazed the first week I was training my rescue Ellie. When I turned for three seconds and when I turned back to Ellie, and she had already moved on to the next best thing.

Dogs' attention span, just like with children, grows with practice and time. Obviously, I wouldn't expect a two-year old child to focus as long as a four-year old. Ellie had never been worked and needed to learn how to focus.

It's important to take a lot of breaks from training sessions and to make the sessions very short. With Ellie, we may have done 2-3 repetitions of an activity, and she was done. Gradually, over six months, she developed the attention span that I would expect from a dog her age.

What are you reinforcing?
From observation of dog owners, I have noticed that they sometimes tend to reinforce the wrong behavior. For example, if the handler is working on *watch*, he must make sure not to treat a sit especially after all the hard work they have put into getting the beautiful *watch* behavior. If you are working on *watch*, the dog does not have to be in a sit.

Another thing I see occasionally, is if a puppy, for example, does a sit and the owner reaches down to treat the puppy, and puppy may jump. It is not good for the owner to deliver the treat if the puppy (or older dog) is jumping. If this happens, then simply move your hand behind your back and wait for your puppy to stand, and then deliver the treat again. Sometimes I will even give the puppy the back of my hand and wait for the jumping to stop before I deliver the treat. I will continue to repeat, turning my hand every time he jumps, and deliver as soon as he stops.

Photo A   *Photo B*

Photo A: Belle is jumping so Michelle turned her hand back.
Photo B: Belle was sitting so Michelle was able to deliver a treat.

What do you do when puppy/dog gets tangled? I have had several different suggestions from mentors on what to do if a dog gets tangled in the leash. One is to allow the puppy or dog to figure out how to disentangle himself, but generally I help them. I asked colleagues of mine what they did, and they responded the same, that they should be untangled. Renea Dahms, author of *Family Companion Dog,* gives her reasons why we should untangle puppy:

- If not helped there is a chance of an unpleasant experience.
- If not helped there is a potential for injury.
- What if the dog never gets untangled? Some dogs are great at it, while others are not. Still others will figure it over time.

What if there is a tension on the leash? Stop and encourage puppy to come toward you, but I wouldn't recommend treating if he comes to you right after having the leash taut—lots of praise and move a few more steps and then reward.

What if puppy just stops after walking a few steps and refuses to move? I will hold the leash taut applying some pressure. I can be one stubborn woman. I have never had a puppy not eventually move. Once puppy moves even slightly, give lots of praise, and move forward. *Be careful* to not create a pattern of him sitting as you wait and then giving him a reward treat. I would encourage you to wait several steps or more before giving a treat.

One of my favorite trainers shared a story at one of her seminars about a marine mammal she was training. She said that on a specific day they had to move all of the mammals into a different, smaller tank so they could clean out the larger tank. One of the mammals decided she didn't want to move into the smaller tank when cued, so the other zookeepers just threw a fish to the other tank so they could get her in quickly and move on to their other end-of-the-day activities. The mammal caught onto this manner of getting a fish, and it became a training pattern. So, when it was her day to move the animals, she cued the behavior, but the mammal just stayed waiting for a treat. She walked away and waited for a bit and re-cued, and the mammal went in, earning a treat. Animals will do what works. Dogs are incredibly intelligent, so it's important to watch and be aware of any pattern behavior like this when training. Remember, treats are a reinforcer. They are a tool in training, and they can reinforce wanted behavior, but sometimes we can inadvertently use them to reinforce unwanted behavior.

Puppy

Once again, leash walking requires patience and team work, but using the appropriate, step-by-step procedures that I recommend with a new puppy or rescue can really reap rewards for a lifetime of pleasurable leash walking experiences for both pet and owner.

CHAPTER 15

REACTIVE DOGS

What if my dog is lunging, barking, and/or growling while walking on the leash?
This book was not written with the intention of working on these issues. However, you can start by applying the impulse control and calming skills at home. I recommend finding a qualified dog trainer or Certified Applied Animal Behaviorist in your area.

With Reactive or Fearful Dogs
Reactive means that your dog is lunging or barking, essentially putting on a grand show for the neighbors, but there is no aggression involved.

In this chapter I have included my recommendations as to what to look for in a professional dog trainer or animal behaviorist. I do believe that the exercises in this book will greatly benefit your training program overall but it is always important to seek help immediately when problems arise as it is always easier to fix problems before they become a habit or even more problematic.

If you are having issues with aggression, a very skilled professional who is knowledgeable in the field may be needed, along with a veterinarian, to help you through the behavior modification program.

There are also some dog trainers that specialize and are very knowledgeable in the field, but sometimes cases are beyond dog trainers and need the help of an animal behaviorist and veterinarian that are able to include medication to modify the negative behavior.

No Laws in the Dog Field

This may come as a surprise to you, but currently in the United States there are no laws restricting who calls themselves dog trainers. This means that anyone that would like to charge for services as an animal trainer can print his or her name on a business card, design an attractive website, and give people "professional" advice. To me, this is a scary thing. There are many families that are dealing with very serious dog aggression issues, which then become a safety issue.

Because there are no laws, I strive to educate all my students so they are knowledgeable when shopping for a trainer. Because of my passion to provide a professional education for dog trainers, I have opened Kenyon Canine Institute. We are in the process of becoming a licensed college. Our long-term goal is to raise the standard for professional dog trainers and to work toward changing the laws. Pet owners will have assurance when hiring a professional dog trainer that the trainer has received a proper education to help them in the same way that they would have confidence in finding a licensed doctor. Kenyon is the first institute of its kind. If you are interested in becoming a professional dog trainer or canine behavior consultant, you can enroll at www.kenyoncanineinstitute.com.

With that being said, we all know that some doctors are better than others. Some have better bedside manners, and others are more committed. These differences in strength are true in the dog training world as well.

What to look for

- When looking for a dog trainer, you must like him/her. After all, this trainer is not just training your dog; he/she is working with you to help you work and interact effectively with your dog.

- Look for someone with credentials. There are no requirements by law, but I think that it says a lot when someone has taken the time to educate themselves. There are several different certifications out there requiring different skill levels. Graduates of Kenyon Canine Institute (KCI) will have a two-year education that covers everything from basic behaviors to very complex behaviors. Other certifications require six weeks of education. It's important to do your research so that you know how much experience and training your trainer has had.

- What types of methods are they using? There are so many different techniques out there. I personally feel strongly that all methods should be based on the humane treatment of an animal, which do not include electric shock collars, metal prong collars, or choke chains. The reason isn't that I am a weak trainer; it is that I have really seen these methods do more harm than good. From most of my observations, these devices unnecessarily confuse the dog. If a person would take some time to truly begin to understand the dog world, I think that he or she would agree with me as well.

- Do the trainers guarantee results? If they do, I would be seriously wary. The BEST dog trainer in the world could not guarantee results with any dog. Let's face it, dogs are living, breathing organisms with a will independent of the owner or trainer. They make their own decisions. There is a difference between a guarantee that you will be happy with the service versus guaranteed results.

- Go with your gut instincts and observe if your dog likes the trainer. Haven't you seen the quote that says if your dog doesn't like someone, you probably shouldn't either? Dogs are good judges of character so it seems, but your gut feeling is as well. Choose someone that you are comfortable with.

- Ask for references and also observe the classes they conduct.

Titles in the Dog World

There are many people currently using terms of qualification such as: "Behavior Counselor," "Animal Psychologist," or "Animal Behaviorist." What do all these terms mean? Who can use which title?

Currently in the United States, there is no law regulating titles in the dog training field, a fact that needs to change. So what this means is that anyone with or without education in the "dog world" can print his or her name on a business card or create a website and start taking business without ever opening a book on dog body language or attending school. Imagine a family with small children hiring a person calling himself or herself a "Behavior Counselor" or even a "Dog Trainer" but has zero educational background and is making suggestions to a family that could potentially affect the well being of their child. Animal behaviorists or dog trainer's often times are dealing with aggression cases that can be life threatening, and having a qualified, certified professional is essential.

What's the difference between an Animal Behaviorist and Dog Trainer?

Dog Trainer

A dog trainer specializes in teaching desired behaviors like sit, come, stay, down, etc. Obviously, even among dog trainers, the skill levels greatly vary. Trainers may help with some issues like separation anxiety, marking, chewing, and perhaps, biting, aggression, etc. There currently are no degree programs in dog training, but this is our goal with Kenyon Canine Institute.

There are recognized and respected certifications in the dog training realm that will help show the level of skill and credentials as a dog trainer.

Animal Behaviorist

An Animal Behaviorist has at least a master's degree from an accredited college or university in an animal science field. Upon completion of a master's or doctoral degree, an Animal Behaviorist can seek certification from an organization.

Some Organizations

Certified Applied Animal Behaviorist

www.certifiedanimalbehaviorist.com

Association of Companion Animal Behavior Counselors

www.animalbehaviorcounselors.org

It is only with this level of education that one can call him/herself an Animal Behaviorist. This person will have an extensive background in behavior and modifying the behavior. When comparing a doctor to someone in the dog training field, the animal behaviorist is a specialist. The animal behaviorist (preferably certified) should receive referrals from a trainer that has been given a case that is beyond his or her ability. Some veterinarians (certainly not most) hold this title which provides a great resource for dog trainers as the veterinarian will not only have the background in animal behavior but also be able to rule out any physical element that might cause the behavior and also prescribe a medication if needed. The number of individuals with an education in this particular field is extremely few.

CHAPTER 16

OTHER GREAT RESOURCES

Protocol for Focus & Relaxation Training*

The purpose of this protocol training is to teach your dog to think through his arousal and to encourage relaxation. The training uses wave-length patterns to get the dog slightly excited and then bring him back down to relaxation. Creating this pattern through the protocol exercises will teach a dog to think through his arousal and be able to focus while continuing to perform a task.

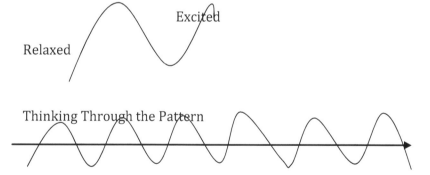

You create this pattern by asking the dog to sit as you exercise small behaviors in front of the dog which encourage his excitement. You reinforce the dog's calm responses to these behaviors as you train. The relaxation protocol increases in the level of difficulty as you move through to the 14th day. The protocol exercise normally takes 7-10 minutes a day.

This is not a sit/stay program. In other words, your dog is allowed to move around during the protocol training. There is no need for corrections; simply re-cue sit for the next exercise. I encourage you to use a mat, towel, or rug to target the dog's location as you work through the relaxation protocol.

Many times dogs experience over arousal at the front door so this location would be a good place to start practicing the protocol. Once you complete the 14-day protocol at the front door, you will begin to re-do the protocol in a different location such as the front porch or backyard.

You are welcome to use your clicker as a marker and reinforce with treats during the protocol exercise. However, if the dog finds the clicker too arousing, the handler should switch to a verbal marker and treats. For some dogs, even the treats are too arousing. If you find this to be your case, use your voice only. Make sure that when you speak to your dog you are using a tone that will encourage relaxation.

You are allowed to talk to your dog during the protocol. Some dogs *need* to hear from you, so while you are silently counting to 15 you can tell them in a tone that promotes relaxation how well they are doing.

If your dog is struggling to accomplish a certain exercise, simply repeat that day's training instead of moving on. Remember to read your dog's body language. You never want a dog to get too aroused during the protocol because it would be counterproductive. If he is showing signs of stress, then I would recommend that you stop training and give your dog a break with something to chew. When you return to the protocol, back up to the last exercise that he was successful in remaining calm, and slow down the speed of progression.

Throughout the protocol exercises, you will look for a relaxed response from your dog. Such signs could be softening of the face, relaxed body position such as going into a down from a sit, relaxed tail wagging, relaxed ears, sighing, yawning, closing his eyes. Anytime you see these behaviors, mark them! You want to reinforce this type of response to strengthen the relaxation behavior.

Go to www.michellehuntting.com/protocol.html to see the video of me demonstrating the protocol for relaxation. Also available on the website is a recorded MP3 of Michelle's Protocol for Focus & Relaxation. I have personally found it easier to listen to the exercises with my MP3 player than reading the exercises from a paper, holding the clicker and treats, and successfully trying to watch my dog.

* This Protocol was created based on Dr. Karen Overall's Protocol for Relaxation located in *Clinical Behavioral Medicine for Small Animals.*

Here is a small sample of Day One:
Sit for 5 seconds
Sit for 15 seconds

This is how I instruct my students to go through this protocol:
Cue a sit, click/treat; count in your mind to 5; if the dog stays in a sit, click/treat.
Cue a sit, click/treat; count in your mind to 15; if your dog stays in a sit, click/treat; if your dog gets up, pause and wait for him to reseat himself, then click/treat.

Day One Exercises
Sit for 10 seconds
Sit for 15 seconds
Sit for 5 seconds
Sit while you shift your body ; rock back and forth twice
Sit for 10 seconds
Sit while you clap your hands once
Sit for 5 seconds
Sit while you take one step back with your left foot and return to original position
Sit while you rock your weight back to your right foot and return weight to center

Sit for 10 seconds
Sit while you take a step to the left
Sit for 3 seconds
Sit while you take a step to the right
Sit while you count aloud to five softly
Sit for 15 seconds
Sit while you clap your hands once
Sit while you take three steps back and return to dog
Sit while you count aloud softly to 10
Sit while you take a step to the left
Sit while you take a step to the right
Sit for 13 seconds
Sit while you count aloud to 20
Sit while you take three steps back and three steps forward

Day Two Exercises
Sit for 5 seconds
Sit while you shift your weight to the left and return weight to center, two times
Sit while you march in place five times
Sit for 20 seconds
Sit while you snap your fingers once
Sit for 3 seconds
Sit while you count aloud to 13
Sit while you take 2 steps to the left
Sit while you take 2 steps to the right
Sit for 20 seconds
Sit while you do the hokey pokey and turn yourself around
Sit for 5 seconds
Sit while you clap once
Sit while you take 5 steps back and 5 steps forward
Sit for 3 seconds
Sit for 10 seconds
Sit while you take steps to move halfway around the left of your dog
Sit for 5 seconds
Sit for 3 seconds

Sit while you take steps to move halfway around the right of your dog
Sit while you clap three times
Sit while you take 4 steps back
Sit for 15 seconds
Sit while you dance in place for 3 seconds
Sit for 20 seconds

Day Three Exercises
Sit for 15 seconds
Sit for 3 seconds
Sit while you count aloud to 20
Sit while you jog in place for 5 seconds
Sit while you walk halfway to the left around your dog
Sit for 10 seconds
Sit while you count aloud to 13
Sit while you clap 5 times
Sit for 3 seconds
Sit while you jog in place
Sit while you take five steps back
Sit for 15 seconds
Sit for 20 seconds
Sit while you take five steps back while clapping
Sit while you walk halfway to the left around your dog
Sit for 20 seconds
Sit while you hum or sing a tune for 10 seconds
Sit as you jog in place for 10 seconds
Sit for 10 seconds
Sit for 10 seconds
Sit for 3 seconds
Sit for 5 seconds

Day Four Exercises
Sit for 5 seconds
Sit for 15 seconds
Sit while you jog to the left three strides
Sit while you jog to the right three strides

Sit while you count aloud to 20
Sit while you do the hokey pokey and turn yourself around
Sit while you walk around your dog from the left
Sit while you walk around your dog from the right
Sit for 20 seconds
Sit for 15 seconds
Sit for 3 seconds
Sit while you hum or sing a tune for 15 seconds
Sit while you jog backwards 5 steps and 5 steps forward
Sit while you move to the left 10 steps and return
Sit while you move to the right 10 steps and 10 steps left
Sit while you count aloud to 10
Sit while you walk all the way around your dog
Sit while you jog to the left 10 strides and jog to the right 10 strides
Sit while you jog to the right 10 strides and jog to the left 10 strides
Sit for 10 seconds
Sit while you do 2 jumping jacks
Sit while you jog back 5 steps while clapping
Sit for 5 seconds

Day Five Exercises
Sit for 20 seconds
Sit for 3 seconds
Sit while you jog backwards, clapping hands, and singing a tune;
return to dog.
Sit while you walk 16 steps back and return to dog
Sit while you take 20 steps to the left of your dog and return to dog
Sit while you take 20 steps to the right of your dog and return to dog
Sit for 15 seconds
Sit for 13 seconds
Sit for 3 seconds
Sit while you walk all the way around your dog
Sit while you jog all the way around our dog
Sit for 10 seconds
Sit while you jog in place for 15 seconds
Sit while you clap 5 times

Sit for 20 seconds
Sit while you count aloud by 5's to 30
Sit for 3 seconds
Sit while you briskly walk backwards 15 steps, clapping, humming a tune; return to dog
Sit for 3 seconds
Sit while you walk all the way around your dog
Sit while you count aloud to 10
Sit for 14 seconds
Sit while you briskly walk away 15 steps and return to dog
Sit for 10 seconds
Sit for 3 seconds
Sit for 5 seconds

Day Six Exercises
Sit for 5 seconds
Sit for 15 seconds
Sit for 3 seconds
Sit while you walk 20 steps away from your dog and return
Sit while you clap 8 times and sing a tune
Sit for 10 seconds
Sit for 3 seconds
Sit while you run in place
Sit while you walk around your dog
Sit while you knock on the wall
Sit for 10 seconds
Sit for 15 seconds
Sit for 20 seconds
Sit while you count aloud to 14
Sit while you walk 20 steps away from your dog, clapping, and singing a tune, and return to dog
Sit while you disappear for 5 seconds and return to dog
Sit for 30 seconds
Sit while you go through a doorway and return to dog
Sit while you walk around your dog while clapping your hands
Sit while you do 3 jumping jacks

Sit while you dance to the left 7 steps and return to dog
Sit while you dance to the right 7 steps and return to dog
Sit for 5 seconds
Sit for 30 seconds

Day Seven Exercises
Sit for 5 seconds
Sit for 20 seconds
Sit while you briskly walk backward, clapping your hands, and return to dog
Sit while singing a tune as you walk around your dog
Sit for 3 seconds
Sit while you walk to the left
Sit while you disappear from the dog's view for 10 seconds
Sit while you disappear from the dog's view for 18 seconds
Sit while you jog to the left 10 steps
Sit while you jog to the right 10 steps
Sit while you sing a 3-second tune
Sit for 5 seconds
Sit while you clap your hands 10 times and count aloud to 10
Sit for 3 seconds
Sit while you disappear from the dog's view for 10 seconds and return to dog
Sit while you disappear from the dog's view for 19 seconds and return to dog
Sit while you do the hokey pokey and you turn yourself around
Sit for 10 seconds
Sit for 15 seconds
Sit while you knock on the wall
Sit while you walk away 20 steps, clapping, and return to dog
Sit while you dance in place 10 seconds
Sit for 3 seconds
Sit while you disappear from dog's view for 15 seconds and return to dog
Sit for 10 seconds
Sit for 15 seconds

Sit for 20 seconds

Day Eight Exercises
Sit for 5 seconds
Sit for 15 seconds
Sit while you walk around your dog singing a tune and clapping
Sit while you jog in place and clap for 5 seconds
Sit while you briskly take 15 steps to the left of your dog
Sit while you briskly take 15 steps to the right of your dog
Sit for 3 seconds
Sit while you sing *Twinkle Twinkle Little Star*
Sit while you count aloud to 20
Sit while you disappear from dog's view for 20 seconds and return to dog
Sit while you walk around your dog
Sit for 5 seconds
Sit while you clap your hands for 15 seconds
Sit while you sit on a couch or chair for 5 seconds
Sit while you jog and clap for 10 seconds
Sit while you disappear from dog's view for 25 seconds and return to dog
Sit for 5 seconds
Sit while you knock on the wall
Sit while you do 4 jumping jacks
Sit for 10 seconds
Sit while you disappear from dog's view for 10 seconds, clapping, and return to dog
Sit for 5 seconds
Sit for 10 seconds
Sit while you disappear from dog's view and sit in a chair, return to dog
Sit for 3 seconds
Sit for 20 seconds

Day Nine Exercises
Sit for 10 seconds
Sit for 5 seconds

Sit while you do the hokey pokey and you turn yourself around
Sit while you clap for 15 seconds
Sit while you count to 25 aloud
Sit while you jog in place for 10 seconds and clap
Sit for 5 seconds
Sit for 8 seconds
Sit for 3 seconds
Sit while you disappear from dog's view for 30 seconds and return to dog
Sit while you knock on the wall
Sit while you walk around your dog as you are clapping
Sit while you jog in place for 15 seconds singing a tune
Sit for 14 seconds
Sit while you sing the alphabet
Sit while you jog around your dog
Sit while you dance to the left 20 feet
Sit while you dance to the right 20 feet
Sit for 3 seconds
Sit while you jog around your dog twice
Sit while you disappear from dog's view for 10 seconds and return to dog
Sit while you disappear from dog's view and sit in chair for 15 seconds and return to dog
Sit for 3 seconds
Sit while you sit on couch or chair for 5 seconds and return to dog
Sit for 10 seconds
Sit while you count aloud for 10 seconds and clap
Sit while you do 2 jumping jacks and touch your toes
Sit for 5 seconds
Sit for 10 seconds
Sit while you do 3 different stretches
Sit for 10 seconds
Sit for 5 seconds

Day Ten Exercises

Sit for 5 seconds

Sit for 10 seconds and clap once

Sit while you jog in place 15 seconds

Sit while you walk around your dog

Sit while you sit on couch or chair for 15 seconds and return to dog

Sit for 3 seconds

Sit while you disappear from dog's view for 30 seconds and return to dog

Sit while you dance in place for 20 seconds

Sit while you disappear from dog's view for 20 seconds

Sit while you disappear from dog's view for 13 seconds and sit in chair

Sit while you walk around your dog, clapping and singing a tune

Sit for 5 seconds

Sit while you knock on the wall 5 times

Sit while you disappear from dog's view for 10 seconds, knock on wall, and return to dog

Sit for 10 seconds

Sit for 15 seconds

Sit while you disappear from dog's view for 10 seconds, clapping and return to dog

Sit for 3 seconds

Sit for 10 seconds

Day Eleven Exercises

Sit for 10 seconds

Sit while you count aloud to 20 and clap

Sit while you turn around

Sit while you jog in place for 15 seconds

Sit while you jog around your dog as you are clapping and singing

Sit for 3 seconds

Sit while you disappear from dog's view for 15 seconds, knock on wall once, and return to dog

Sit while you sing *Twinkle Twinkle Little Star*

Sit for 4 seconds

Sit while you disappear from dog's view for 20 seconds and sit in chair; return to dog

Sit while you sit on couch or chair

Sit while you knock on wall 6 times

Sit while you do 4 jumping jacks

Sit for 3 seconds

Sit while you disappear from dog's view for 10 seconds, knock on wall 3 times, and return to dog

Sit while you do 3 stretches

Sit while you bend over and touch your toes

Sit while you do the hokey pokey and you turn yourself around

Sit for 3 seconds

Sit while you sing a tune and turn yourself around

Sit while you clap for 20 seconds

Sit while you count aloud for 10 seconds

Sit while you jog in place 15 seconds

Sit while you walk around your dog

Sit for 15 seconds

Sit for 20 seconds

Sit while you disappear from dog's view for 15 seconds and return to dog

Sit for 10 seconds

Sit for 15 seconds

Day Twelve Exercises

Sit for 5 seconds

Sit for 15 seconds

Sit while you dance in place for 20 seconds

Sit while you jog in place for 15 seconds

Sit while you jog to left of your dog 15 steps

Sit while you jog to the right of your dog 15 steps

Sit while you sit on couch for 10 seconds

Sit while you briskly walk backwards, clapping and counting aloud 15 steps, and return to dog

Sit while you briskly walk around your dog

Sit for 20 seconds

Sit for 30 seconds

Sit while you disappear from dog's view for 25 seconds and return to dog

Sit while you disappear from dog's view for 15 seconds and knock 5 times, and return to dog

Sit while you sing *Twinkle Tinkle Little Star*

Sit for 3 seconds

Sit while you do 4 jumping jacks

Sit while you clap for 10 seconds

Sit while you disappear from dog's view for 10 seconds and sit in chair and return to dog

Sit while you walk around your dog

Sit while you Pledge Allegiance to the Flag and walk backwards 10 steps, walk to the left of your dog 5 steps, and walk to the right of your dog 5 steps, and return to dog

Sit while you jump up and down 3 times

Sit while you knock on the wall 7 times

Sit for 10 seconds

Sit for 5 seconds

Sit for 15 seconds

Day Thirteen Exercises

Sit for 10 seconds

Sit for 15 seconds while you sing a little

Sit while you jog in place 10 seconds

Sit while you jog in place and knock on wall 3 times

Sit for 3 seconds

Sit while you count aloud to 23

Sit while you clap your hands and count aloud to 23

Sit for 3 seconds

Sit while you disappear from dog's view for 15 seconds, knock on wall, and return to dog

Sit while you jog to disappear from dog's view for 10 seconds, knock on wall, and return to dog

Sit for 10 seconds

Sit while you do 6 jumping jacks and briskly walk around your dog

Sit for 6 seconds

Sit while you clap your hands singing part of the National Anthem

Sit while you back away from you dog 24 steps

Sit for 10 seconds

Sit while you disappear from dog's view for 20 seconds, knock on the wall once, and return to dog

Sit while you touch your toes and do a little dance for 10 seconds

Sit while you walk around your dog and knock on wall once

Sit for 5 seconds

Sit while you briskly walk to the left of your dog 15 steps

Sit while you jog about 15 steps to the right of your dog as you sing

Sit for 3 seconds

Sit while you disappear from dog's view for 10 seconds

Sit while you sit on the couch

Sit for 5 seconds

Sit for 20 seconds

Day Fourteen Exercises

Sit for 5 seconds

Sit for 15 seconds

Sit while you touch your toes and sing a song for 10 seconds

Sit while you disappear from dog's view for 25 seconds and return to dog

Sit while you walk around your dog as you sing

Sit while you clap for 15 seconds

Sit while you jog away from dog 15 steps and return to dog

Sit while you jog around your dog

Sit while you disappear from dog's view for 40 seconds and return to dog

Sit while you disappear from dog's view for 10 seconds and return to dog

Sit for 5 seconds

Sit while you sit on couch for 15 seconds

Sit while you disappear, clapping for 10 seconds, and return to dog

Sit while you disappear and knock on wall 3 times and return to dog

Sit while you do 3 jumping jacks

Sit for 20 seconds

Sit while you take three steps to the left, singing and clapping, and return to dog

Sit while you take three steps to the right, singing and clapping, and return to dog

Sit while you jog in place for 20 seconds

Sit while you sing *Twinkle Twinkle Little Star* and walk around your dog

Sit while you clap your hands for 15 seconds

Sit for 3 seconds

Sit while you disappear from dog's view for 30 seconds and return to dog

Sit while you disappear from dog's view for 15 seconds, knock on the wall 5 times, and return to dog

Sit for 5 seconds

Sit while you clap and jog in place for 10 seconds

Sit while you sit on the floor for 5 seconds

Sit while you walk around your dog

Sit while you walk away from dog 25 steps, and return to dog

Sit while you sing, clap, and walk away from dog 25 steps and return to dog

Sit for 5 seconds

Sit for 20 seconds

Sit for 30 seconds

Articles

The remainder of this chapter contains resources from knowledgeable sources. I felt very strongly that this information be included in my book to make it complete. I have concluded each article with their professional contact information. These articles belong to each individual author.

Food and Treat Content by Kim Matsko

"Oh, c'mon Mom, just one piece of candy!" How many times have you heard that? Or, even said those words yourself when you were a kid? Do you cave and let them have that piece of candy? Or do you resist and offer them a piece of fruit instead because you know fruit is a healthier choice than candy?

Now, how many of you know that same pleading look in your dog's eyes? The one that says, "C'mon Mom, just one little treat!" Those dark, soulful eyes begging you for that colorful, sausage-looking treat or the one that looks like a strip of bacon. How can you say "no"? Do you cave in and give the morsel? Do you even know what's in it?

Scenarios such as this are all-too common in both the human and the pet worlds. We are taught from a very young age that nutrition is the foundation of health. The same holds true for dogs. And just as parents take responsibility for what they give their children to eat, it is also our duty, as pet parents, to know and understand what we are feeding our dogs to ensure that we are optimizing their nutrition and offering the best quality nutrition we can.

One might believe that any commercial pet product on the market must certainly be healthy enough for our pets to consume; otherwise, we assume, it wouldn't be sold. Tell that to the hundreds of dogs who have died and the thousands of dogs who became ill after eating chicken jerky treats imported from China. The unfortunate fact of the matter is commercial pet products can be rife with poor quality ingredients, artificial preservatives, artificial food colorings, and animal byproducts that may very well include euthanized animals and even road kill.

It is vitally important to our pet's health to have a basic understanding of their ancestry and biological needs so that we may, in turn, provide the best diet and nutrition possible to promote health, wellness, and longevity. Many of us know that dogs are direct descendants of the gray wolf, but few of us realize just how closely related they truly are. Most sources agree that dogs and wolves share at least 99 per cent of their mitochondrial DNA with one another. Hard to believe that a Chihuahua or a Bulldog is that biologically similar to the gray wolf, right? However, once people accept the reality of that common link, doesn't it stand to reason that their dietary needs would be similar?

Choosing the appropriate food can be a challenge because there are many different types of foods and treats in today's pet food market and within those types, hundreds and hundreds of different brands. The type and brand of food and treats you offer your pet can greatly impact its overall health and well-being. In today's market, you can select food ranging anywhere from dry dog kibble to frozen raw food and anything in between including canned food, moist pouches, dehydrated food, and freeze-dried food. Some pet owners even opt to cook their own food or prepare their own raw diets from home. However, it should be noted that doing so requires careful consideration and consultation with your holistic veterinarian to ensure you are preparing a complete and balanced diet that is not devoid of essential vitamins and minerals. Most pet professionals agree that feeding an unbalanced home cooked diet can be far worse for your pet even than feeding the lowest quality commercial dry food.

Once you've settled on what type of food you feel is going to provide the best nutrition for your pet, you must then evaluate the ingredients in the different brands. More and more pet parents are realizing how important it is to feed a more natural diet and avoid certain ingredients in pet food which may include corn, wheat, soy, animal by-products, artificial preservatives, and artificial food colorings. Some pet parents are even looking for food sourced from free range meats raised without the use of hormones and antibiotics.

And pet parents are also becoming more aware of the frequency in which genetically modified organisms (GMO) are used in both human and pet foods and are demanding products that do not contain GMO's. After you familiarize yourself with a few different brands of food that meet the criteria of ingredients you are looking for, you should then do some further investigation to find out where the food is made, including the country and the manufacturing facility, where the ingredients originate from, and if that company or manufacturing facility has a history of recalls. The latter of these can create a whole other problem itself because of the risk and danger of contaminated products.

I, personally, feed a commercial frozen raw diet to my four bulldogs. Based on the research I've done and my personal beliefs on how pets should be fed, a commercial raw diet is the best fit for my lifestyle. I would love to be able to make my own balanced raw diet from local, fresh, free-range meat sources and organically grown vegetables and fruits. However, time does not allow me the ability to do this to the extent I would want to. I also have certain limiting health factors among my population of bulldogs which require me to feed specific diets containing (or not containing) certain ingredients, and a raw diet fits the needs of my dogs best.

For those of you interested in feeding a frozen raw diet, there are a number of excellent commercial brands of raw food in today's market, and more are popping up all the time. Some of the more popular brands you may encounter in your search include:

Aunt Jeni's®
Bravo! ®
Instinct (Nature's Variety) ®
K-9 Kraving®
Northwest Naturals®
OC Raw®
Primal®
Stella & Chewy's®
Vital Essentials®

You may also recall that I mentioned freeze-dried and dehydrated diets previously. These are diets that are either cooked or raw, and the moisture has been removed from the food through the processes of either freeze-drying or dehydrating. Preparation and feeding of these diets is quite convenient as you simply add water to rehydrate the diet to assure your pet is getting an appropriate amount of moisture in the diet. There are a variety of high quality, commercially available freeze-dried and dehydrated diets at your local pet supply shops which may include:

Dr. Harvey's®
Grandma Lucy's®
Orijen®
Primal®
Sojos®
Stella & Chewy's®
The Honest Kitchen®
Ziwi Peak®

It is important to realize that not everyone is in a position to feed a frozen raw, freeze-dried, or dehydrated diet, and it could be for any number of reasons. If dry kibble is what works best for you and your pet, please be aware that dry food is where we see the greatest variation in quality so that it becomes extremely important to know what you are feeding your dog. There are so many dry foods in today's market, so I will simply mention a few of my personal favorites who stand behind their quality and who have never had a recall. Those include:

Acana®
Annamaet®
Canine Caviar®
Earthborn®
Fromm®
Merrick®
Orijen®
VeRUS®

Several of the dry food companies listed above also offer canned or moist diets which provide some additional benefits if fed solely or added to dry kibble. Dogs have at least a 70 per cent moisture requirement in their diet in addition to their normal water intake, so the added moisture content in canned diets can be really beneficial. It is important to note that some canned food or moist diets are not complete and balanced and are intended for supplemental feeding or mixing with another form of balanced diet.

Much of what you search for in food will hold true for treats as well, especially if you are doing a lot of treating for the purposes of training. While there can be some really poor quality foods out there, there are an equal number or more poor quality treats on the market as in the case of the sad situation of imported Chinese chicken jerky treats. Semi-moist treats are often very popular for training because they are palatable and don't take a lot of time to chew, but it is important to evaluate the ingredients as many of these treats have added sugars to help increase palatability but can have an undesirable effect during training sessions, including excitability. Treats high in sugar also promote weight gain, so once again, it becomes extremely important to read the ingredients and be aware of what you are feeding your pets. Some of the more popular training treats we see used include:

Cloud Star Tricky Trainers®
Fromm Four Star Low Fat Dog Treats®
Max & Ruffy's Mini Bites®
Salmon Paws®
Sojos Good Dog Treats®
Wet Noses Little Stars®
Zukes Mini Naturals®

Some dogs who are finicky or not as food or treat motivated may require a little more creativity during training sessions to find what drives them to perform.

So, what do you do when those soulful, brown eyes are staring at you clearly begging for that tasty morsel? Do you give it? Sure, go right ahead. Once you have done your homework and selected an appropriate dietary regimen for your best pal, there's no reason in the world why you shouldn't indulge him in moderation just as you might indulge yourself or your two-legged children. Life is about balance, but it is fundamentally important to provide the best nutrition possible for your furry family members.

Kim Matsko is the owner of Natural Pet Essentials® in Charlottesville, Virginia. www.cvillepetessentials.com

Socialization for Success by Jennifer Shryock

Families are told from the beginning to "socialize" their new dog or puppy. This is wonderful advice and is an important step towards success for a new dog or puppy when done properly. Here are some tips for socialization success!

Pack for success! Before you go anywhere with your pup or new dog be sure to think and plan ahead. I carry a small backpack for tools we may need while out. Each item either meets a need or is a great reward or distraction for situations I might encounter. Here are some essentials.

1. Potty bags & wipes (for me)
2. 3 varieties of treats (low value to HIGH) have plenty
3. Water bowl & bottle
4. Toys, ball, tug and squeaky
5. Clicker & target stick

Short and sweet! It is a great idea to take your puppy to many different environments but keep the visits short and comfortable. Instead of taking your puppy to an entire soccer game your child is participating in, take your dog on a short visit when you are able to focus on your dog and leave after a few minutes of observing and taking in the activity. Often families with great intentions will overdo it. When it comes to positive and enjoyable socialization less is more! Too much time and the puppy may shutdown, zone out or possibly develop a negative association from the experience. Consider the environment, the activity level, and the number of people that will touch your puppy. All of this is sensory intake for a little pup to handle. Keeping these experiences short and sweet are keys for comfort that allow them to remain positive.

Mix it up! It is easy to keep to our routines and include our new puppy or dog. This however can limit the dog's socialization opportunities. It is important to experience new places, sights and sounds together so that your puppy learns to trust you and is comfortable in a variety of settings and situations. Ex: Have a quick "happy visit" to your vet. No exam just a visit where treats happen. We normally would not do this but it is incredibly helpful for your dog or puppy to ease their times when you do need a visit.

Remember observe your dog/puppy and keep it short and sweet.

I spy! I like to think of odd things my puppy or new dog can see or experience. Farm animals, noisy odd-looking trucks, people pushing strollers etc. Make a list of as many different looking things that you can expose your puppy/dog to. Then begin to slowly check them off on your outings. Always plan for short sessions with yummy treats. Observe your puppy/dog for signs of stress or uncertainty. Having an option to leave is a must so that you do not overdo it. Ex: Go outside with treats or a favorite toy just before you expect the mail to be delivered. Sometimes we meet the delivery person and sometimes not. The idea is that your dog gets used to the rumble of the truck and seeing the person coming and going.

Weather happens!! Nothing is worse than a dog that won't potty on a rainy day! One thing many people do not often think about is having their dog walk and potty on different surfaces and textures. This can lead to long-term challenges when it comes to some dogs and weather changes. Exposing your dog to different textures and surfaces is helpful and important! Get them used to going "potty" on different surfaces and weather conditions. This truly pays off long term. Dogs that are not exposed to these new textures and conditions often will have problems down the road adapting when they need to.

Sensitive ears! It is so important to exposure your puppy or new dog to different types of sounds. Many dogs are sound sensitive and short bits of exposure in a safe environment can help them. There are many sound CD's or digital downloads can help with sounds like dogs barking, kids playing, storms etc. This can be a great way to help your dog become familiar with these unique sounds so that when they happen naturally your dog has had some positive encounters. I used to keep frozen goodies on hand for thunder storms. We made a "thunder party." For the pups. Be creative and have fun!

Kids all around! Socialization around all different ages is important. Dogs that have not been exposed to children, babies and awkward toddlers may be very uncomfortable or fearful. When visiting a park or place for socialization purposes please always observe your dog for stress signals. Keep in mind that interaction between your dog and unfamiliar children is not necessary. When it comes to children your dog needs to know that they can defer to you for help. Always give your dog an out when you sense or observe stress or discomfort. You can hand a child or parent a treat to drop on the ground and allow your puppy or dog to eat it. Bring along a favorite toy for the child to hand to your dog or toss. Always keep in mind that you are your dog's advocate and that you decide who and how interaction will be done in all situations based on what is best for your dog.

Socialization exercises allow you to really truly get to know your puppy or new dog. Actively observing your dogs on your outings for socialization is the best way to ensure less stress and more success. It is true that exposure to many situations is important but knowing if your dog is enjoying these experiences or is ready for a break is essential for long-term success! So, get your list and pack your puppy bag and have fun!

Jennifer Shryock is the founder of Dogs & Storks®, Baby & Dog Connection™, and owner of Family Paws Parent Education®. www.familypaws.com

Three Ways I Used a Spiritual Approach and Improved my Dog Training Business by Karen Palmer

My name is Karen Palmer and I am a mom, yoga instructor, Law of Attraction Coach, and Reiki Master. I have helped people for many years overcome challenges and improve their lives. Three years ago I ventured into a new territory. I expanded my non-profit business to include animal advocacy and helping educate elementary school children to be kind to animals and each other. I dreamed of working with animals and especially helping animals that were abused and abandoned. I am a survivor of domestic abuse and I wanted to help animals that I felt were misunderstood. I will explain how I used the techniques that helped people improve the lives of many unwanted animals. If you would like to reach out to me please visit www.positivelypetsandkids.com

The Law of Attraction is the name given to the belief that "like attracts like" and that by focusing on positive or negative thoughts, one can bring about positive or negative results. This belief is based upon the idea that people and their thoughts are both made from pure energy, and the belief that like energy attracts like energy. I decided to try this with the dogs I was training and here are some of the amazing results I saw.

Brittany was seven years old and Bella was three when I started walking them a little over a year ago. Vicki explained the reason the dogs had not been walked was because she had severe arthritis and other complicated health issues. I was hesitant at first, but I knew if I asked for help it would come. I prayed, "God if I can be helpful please give me the strength to help this family." I had the feeling that the law of attraction would help. I need to see the results and believe in both of these dogs; so they could believe in themselves.

I felt that wave of peace that I was getting accustomed to feeling when I trust my inner guidance. I knew this would be another gift if I chose to accept it. This was a great test of faith for me, and wow, am I glad I did. The first day I went over to Vicki's house, she greeted me at the door. She was so sweet and kind and I knew we would be friends. Both dogs were in the garage when I arrived, I heard them barking and jumping against the door. They sounded scary. I quickly said a prayer to stay calm and assertive. I was peaceful but I established strong leadership qualities.

The dogs came out of the garage and calmly sniffed me. They both listened as I told them to sit. Vicki was shocked and I was surprised myself, but with God all things are possible. Vicki told me Brittany had issues with other dogs and would sometimes attack Bella.

Bella is a beautiful full bred Dalmatian but she was born all black with white spots. The breeders were horrible people and because they didn't think anyone would pay for her and they tried to drown her. She survived. They tried to strangle her; this was why she had severe anxiety and fear of strangers. She was saved by "The Dalmatian Rescue Team" after the breeders abandoned her in Los Angeles traffic.

Bella was extremely scared of everyone and the rescue team knew she would need a special home. The rescue team called Vicki and her husband John and they decided to adopt Bella. Both Brittany and Bella had been abused and neglected before John and Vicki adopted them. They were left starving in the streets in an area where there was a lot of traffic.

Brittany adapted well to having a forever home. She loved all the attention and love she was receiving and forgot all the horrible experiences she had been through. Bella unfortunately was not adapting well; she was still afraid of everything. She was terrified of the vacuum cleaner, loud trucks, and motorcycles. She was horrified by the statues in their backyard and would crawl up to them and bark horrendously. I knew this would be a challenging case but I was not alone.

I went right to work with Brittany and helped her understand loving leadership roles. She loved it! I could tell she was happy to have someone   believe in her. She really wanted someone to give her directions and we enjoyed our time together. She enjoyed learning new skills and was very proud of herself. The training gave her peace of mind and we developed an amazing bond. The training was a success and she was excellent on our walks.

She learned to walk through traffic and stayed close to me. She was not afraid. We spent many hours exploring the beautiful place we live in. She stopped being aggressive toward other dogs and Bella. Bella was becoming more confident too. She was comfortable walking through town and trusted me. This was just one of many examples I have witnessed as a dog trainer. Sometimes animals that have been abused need us to believe in them. Using the law of attraction helps animals in some of the same ways it helps humans.

2. **Reiki healing** is a natural therapy that gently balances life energies and brings health and well-being to the recipient. I have seen miracles using this healing modality on several of my human clients and decided to experiment using it on animals after I became certified. Here is a true story about a very special dog who I am still working with and we are looking to find his forever home.

Darby: My dear friend C.C called me. She is the owner and founder of www.happyendingsanimalrescuesanctuary.org; an incredible animal rescue organization where I volunteer. I help dogs with intense behavior issues heal their issues and become the amazing dogs they truly are.

My friend called me because she saved the life of a dog named Darby. He spent his life being used as dog bait in dog fighting. He was muzzled and attacked to build up the dogs that were fighting. He was left to die, tied to a tree with no food or water for six days. One of the neighbors contacted C.C. and she went to rescue him. She saved his life got him to her vet and he survived but was very aggressive. C.C. called me and asked me to start to work with Darby. I meditated and prayed; asking to be helpful to this beautiful dog. He is a Catahoula and Australian Sheppard. I knew God was leading me to help this amazing dog. The first moment we met there was an incredible connection. He looked at me so deeply.

I could feel he knew I was there to help. I prayed and felt guided to do some Reiki and energy work with him. I placed my hand on his heart and I felt all his pain and saw visions of the horrible abuse he endured. Tears filled my eyes as I remembered the abuse I had suffered through all those years ago. It was the most magical moment of pure love and we developed a mutual trust and respect like I had never felt before. I loved working with Darby; he is such a smart dog and really wants to please.

In one week he was doing awesome, I was teaching him how to play ball and he loved going for rides in my truck. I took him to the park and started to introduce him to strangers. He completely trusts me and loves to meet new people. He knows I will never hurt him or bring him to any danger. He is really doing great but needs to find a program that offers rehabilitation with other dogs.

I am starting a blog and Facebook® page for Darby to give him the best chance. The sanctuary is a wonderful place but he really needs to be able to run and get lots of exercise and he needs help with socializing. He is very loved at the sanctuary and enjoys the attention and great care he receives. Darby has confirmed for me again that dogs are unconditional, forgiving, they live in the moment, and just spread joy. I have learned so much working with these phenomenal animals.

3. Mindfulness—Benefits of Mindfulness

Being mindful literally lowers your stress level. Health Psychologist says mindfulness decreases levels of the stress hormone cortisol. Mindfulness makes people more compassionate according to a study done in "The Journal of Psychological Science". Decreases feelings of depression; research from the University Of California, Los Angeles found that applying mindfulness helped decreases loneliness among the elderly and boosted their health. Lowered depression risk in teens according to a study from University of Leuven, the practice of mindfulness could help teens experience less stress, anxiety, and depression.

According to a survey of psychologists conducted by Consumer's Report, mindfulness training was considered an excellent strategy for weight loss. The mindful walks you take with your dog will benefit you and your dog.

The University of Utah's study found that mindfulness training helps control our emotions and moods. It also helps us sleep better.

I will be sharing on my blog and in my videos many techniques that will help you in your practice of mindfulness. I hope you will give it a try and you will see the benefits for yourself. I became a yoga instructor because yoga saved my life. I have learned to use the practice of mindfulness in everything I do. I observe and do not judge. It has helped me in all areas of my life and I know it will help you too. I am dedicated to your success. I truly believe in you and I am here to be truly helpful please let me know if I can be of service to you and your pet. I encourage you to try mindfulness here are a few exercises and please apply them when you are out walking with your dog.

Instructions
1. Practice mindfulness while walking. Mindfulness means being in the moment without ruminating about the past or trying to plan out the future. Start by focusing your awareness on the physical experience of walking. Feel the ground under your feet; be aware of body sensations; notice how the air feels on your skin.
2. Pay attention to what you are thinking about. Whether you're planning a grocery list or prioritizing your work tasks for the next day notice this and let the thoughts go. Gently return your attention to the experience of walking.
3. Watch your dog for pointers on mindfulness. Dogs do not ruminate about the past, nor do they try to figure out the future. A dog on a walk is completely focused on the task of walking, which means absorbing as much of the experience in the moment as possible. Your dog will not miss much along the way. He will notice every squirrel and chipmunk, every sound, every smell. All his senses are completely engaged in the business of going for a walk.
4. Introduce a deep breathing practice. Inhale deeply and slowly, and exhale slowly and fully as you walk. Concentrate on your breath flowing in and out. Alternate several of these deep breaths with normal breathing.
5. Experience your surroundings. Look at the plants and trees, the colors of the leaves, the quality of the light, the sounds of the birds and the insects. Combine this with your deep breathing practice by inhaling your experience.
6. Observe your dog again for more tips. Your dog is definitely incorporating a breathing practice into the walk. Blades of grass are noticed and scrutinized, and the experience of that moment is inhaled deeply and fully. By experiencing the world through the breath, your dog is living very much in the moment.

I have learned many spiritual lessons from these incredible animals. I ask myself daily *WHAT IF* every human believed the reasons they are here on Earth, is to be unconditional, forgiving, live in the moment and to spread joy. This is what the dogs have taught me and I live my life this way and feel so grateful.

Scent Detection; a Game, a Sport by Barb Ruehl

Scent Detection (or Nose Work, or K9 Nose Work®) is a game that has been developed into a canine sport. It is based on the job that professional K9's and handlers perform at borders and ports of entry every day. Those dogs are trained to search for drugs or explosives or items that might harm the agricultural business in this country; most sport scent detection dogs are trained to find tiny amounts of specific essential oils.

The activity of Nose Work has a lot of benefits. It's fun for the dog, and fun – and amazing – for the handler and others who observe the searches. Only one dog is allowed in the search area at any time; dog reactive dogs learn quickly that they are 100% safe. The dogs learn to love to search among containers, and to solve puzzles to find their rewards. That puzzle solving works their brain and tires out most dogs. There's another important benefit – as the dog learns the game and comes to love it, most dogs display an increase in confidence, even dogs that start out very skittish and concerned in new environments.

There are a variety of methods available for teaching Nose Work. Some work for a specific type of dog – for example, a professional scent detection dog which was selected for its high drive and enthusiasm in play would probably excel in training situations that rewarded with a lot of tug games and retrieves. But a small beagle that was recently rescued from a puppy mill situation may shut down when around that amount of intensity.

That doesn't mean that the scared little beagle cannot learn scent detection - it just means that another training method will work better for this dog. The National Association of Canine Scent Work (or NACSW™) has developed a method of training K9 Nose Work® that will work for any dog. They teach this method to instructors & certify those that complete the training (an instructor that has successfully completed the training is called a CNWI, or Certified Nose Work Instructor; someone still working to achieve that title is an ANWI, or Associate Nose Work Instructor.)

Besides certifying instructors, NACSW also sanctions Odor Recognition Tests and Nose Work Trials for the sport of K9 Nose Work® and titles dogs that complete those Trials successfully. You can get more information about NACSW™, the rule book for Nose Work or a list of Certified Instructors at their website (www.nacsw.net).

The NACSW method of training Scent Work starts by determining each dog's highest value reward, whether a toy, a dog treat, or some other food like cheese or chicken or liver. We begin by confirming the dog will take the treat out of a cardboard carton. Usually we'll tuck in the flaps so that they won't move around and scare the dog just starting out. Some dogs are afraid even then, so we may turn the carton on its side or take a carton lid or just a piece of cardboard to represent the carton. Petite breeds or dogs that are very environmentally sensitive can benefit from starting out using carton lids, and gradually move them into cartons set on their side, and then cartons with no flaps, and then cartons with flaps.

After the instructor has determined that the dog will take treats from a carton (or has switched to lids or a piece of cardboard to start), they place the reward into a carton and place that carton on the floor, amidst a half dozen empty cartons. The first few times this happens, the dog is allowed to watch the box placement, but the third or fourth time, the dog will be distracted either by the handler or the instructor, as the box with the treat is placed. The dog may still need to be encouraged through the cartons, but will find the treat and self-reward. Each time the dog rewards, the handler should step in and gently remove the carton from beneath the dog's nose, rather than pulling the dog off the carton.

The best time to end the round of searches (or any subsequent round of searches) is while the dog is still very enthusiastic about continuing. Down time in a crate is encouraged. If a crate is not available, the dog should be moved to another location so that the only dog in the search area is the dog that is actively working.

Once the dog is pulling toward the cartons enthusiastically, use the cartons to complicate the search. Set another carton over ½ of the hide carton (with the reward visible). Later, cover the reward with the second carton. Release the flaps on the reward carton, and gradually work the hides so that the dog has to push past the flaps to reach the reward. Set a carton upside down on top of another carton and add a small amount of elevation to the hide. Some dogs can deal with these complications on the first day of playing 'the game' – others will take longer. But they will all have a lot of fun on the journey.

Over several practice sessions, the 'puzzle solving' can become more complicated. The instructor can also add more cartons or other containers such as buckets or traffic cones. The dogs can be allowed to work off lead, or the handler can practice their lead handling – allowing the dog to move through the containers.

The more practice sessions can be videoed and reviewed, the more the handler can learn to look for cues – for example, some dogs slow down when they get in scent; others may speed up. Most dogs breathe more deeply (some breathe quite loudly) when in scent. The dog may perform a head snap toward the source of the odor. If moving at a quick pace, they may come to an abrupt stop. Reviewing videos regularly is a great help to the handler. Look for a class that makes it a practice to video searches when it's possible.

Following these steps will give a dog a solid foundation in K9 Nose Work®, and if the team elects to work with a Certified Nose Work Instructor, adding additional environments (called 'elements') and the dog's target scents can happen quickly.

Learn to read your dog and enjoy observing his or her olfactory skills; trust your dog and you will be constantly amazed.

Barb Reuhl is a professional trainer in Downer Grove, Illinios. www.noseworkdogs.com

The Art of Taking the Treat Sweetly by Renea Dahms

Not all dogs understand the subtleties of treat taking; there are gators in our midst. The simplest way to help your dog learn to be sweet when taking the treat, is to allow his/her own actions to dictate the consequences. This is not always easy.

First start out with a lower value treat to keep arousal low. Your dog's food may work well for this.

You also need to be in a low distraction area, again to keep arousal low.

Offer your dog the treat. Should s/he bite hard, simply move your hand back and away from the dog. Be sure you still have the treat and say nothing.

Offer your dog the treat again. You should note your dog attempt less enthusiastically to grab the treat. If your dog is still using a lot of teeth, again remove your hand with the treat, say nothing.

Again offer your dog the treat. As your dog attempts to get the treat, use an open hand so your dog can get the treat without catching fingers. You need to allow the dog to get the treat to avoid frustration and/or simply giving up and losing interest in getting it.

You will repeat these steps of taking your hand away for toothy grabs and offering the treat on your open hand.

When you are offering the treat, any softer attempt should be reinforced by allowing your dog to eat the treat. The goal is for him/her to learn that his/her actions drive the consequence. Too hard of a bite means no treat, while softer use of the mouth equals good stuff.

When your dog is using a softer mouth, you can up the ante by using a treat the dog considers of higher value. You may need to start again, but should quickly be back to a softer mouth grab.

As you progress, you can begin adding distraction. Go the yard, the park, dog class, add people or other animals (if available/applicable) and anything you can think of that is not too stressful but will increase the arousal level of your dog.

Remember it is important you do not scold your dog or punish in ways that are harmful. Simply removing the treat (a time out of sorts) is enough for the dog to begin learning how s/he can lose access to the treat, as well as how to adjust to gain it.

Renea Dahms is the owner of Pawsitively Unleashed in Stevens Point, Wisconsin. www.pawsitivelyunleashed.com

Using Massage for Dogs by Kristen McCartney

For most, the term "massage therapy" is synonymous with relaxation. While it is very relaxing, there are so many health benefits of massage therapy for both humans and canines alike. While massage therapy is never meant to replace veterinary care, it can be very beneficial for dogs whether they are in perfect health or suffering from chronic conditions such as arthritis or hip dysplasia. Because so many major systems of the body are either directly or indirectly impacted by massage therapy, the results can be seen in dogs of all breeds, ages, and activity levels.

To get an idea of how massage therapy can benefit even the healthiest of canines, let's first take a look at how massage therapy affects the entire body. Aside from the muscles themselves, some of the body's most intricate systems are impacted by massage. The circulatory system, for example, is stimulated greatly during a massage session. This in turn creates an increase in the flow of healthy blood and oxygen not only to all the muscles of the body, but also to the organs. Along with the circulatory system, the lymphatic system also receives the benefits of this increased flow throughout the body. Just as in humans, a dog's lymphatic system has many roles in maintaining a healthy body. It is responsible for helping to absorb and transport fatty acids from the digestive system to the rest of the body, as well as transporting white blood cells throughout the body. Since white blood cells act as the body's defense against disease, infection, and foreign bodies, a well-functioning lymphatic system is essential to preventing illness.

Another system impacted by massage therapy is the myofascial system. Surprisingly few people are familiar with myofascia (also referred to as fascia), even though a human's myofascia is strikingly similar to that of most animals. The myofascial system can be thought of as a thin, continuous, flexible net; it covers the entire body and even weaves itself in between muscles, blood vessels, and nerves. It not only provides structure and support to the entire body, but also aids in the filtering of toxins and maintaining water for the body. Because this tissue is continuous, any stress in myofascia in one area of the body can have effects on every other part of the body as well. Over time, stress, injury, and adhesions in the myofascia can lead to restricted movement and even abnormal gaits in your dog. A massage therapist will often use myofascial massage (also called myofascial release) in addition to regular massage to help maintain a healthy myofascial system and prevent mobility issues.

Even if your dog is in very good health, these benefits of massage can help to maintain that level of health, especially if your dog is very active or competing in events such as agility or flyball. By increasing the health and elasticity of the muscles, injuries such as sprains and pulls are less likely to occur, and even in the event of such an injury, recovery time can be greatly reduced.

In the case of dogs who are suffering from chronic conditions such as arthritis, hip, or elbow dysplasia, it is always important to have the dog examined by a veterinarian before consulting with a massage therapist. This way, the massage therapist can be well informed of the severity of the dog's condition, as well as any other contributing health factors. While these chronic conditions can never be fully cured, there are massage techniques that can help make the dog more comfortable and help maintain a higher level of mobility. It is common for dogs suffering from these conditions to modify their gait in order to ease the pain caused by moving the effected limb or joint. Over time, doing this has several effects. First, although it may relieve some of the pressure from the painful joint, it also transfers added pressure to other joints and muscles of the body as they have to compensate for the lack of use of the effected joint. In hip dysplasia, for example, the shoulders often begin to bear most of the pressure that the hips would normally absorb. Secondly, this avoided use of the painful area can cause loss of muscle mass, reduced range of motion (ROM), and shortening of the muscles associated with the painful joint.

By gently working on the muscles surrounding the affected area, a massage therapist can help to restore the muscles that your dog has avoided using and relieve soreness, as well as relieve the tension that has been added to the compensating muscles. By addressing all the muscles being affected, normal muscle balance can begin to return to the body. Many massage therapists will also incorporate some passive (assisted) stretches for the dog, which will further help to increase ROM and promote healthy muscle growth and elasticity. Combined with the increased circulation brought about by massage therapy, all these things can help your dog enjoy greater mobility and comfort despite their chronic condition.

These same techniques can also be applied to a dog who is recovering from an acute injury or surgery. Often times during the recovery period, muscles can become stiff and even atrophy from lack of use, as well as be impacted by the formation of scar tissue. The use of massage therapy can help to ensure a recovering canine can get back on their feet more easily, and avoid any prolonged effects from their injury.

Aside from the physical benefits of massage therapy, there can also be behavioral benefits. Massage therapy can help a timid or fearful dog become more comfortable with human touch, as well as help to socialize them by teaching them that having their paws, ears, and other areas of the body handled is no big deal. This can help a nervous dog gain more confidence in their daily life, and be more comfortable around their human companions. Hyperactive dogs can benefit, as well. Regular massage therapy can not only help a hyper dog learn to relax, but can also release tensions that owners may not even realize are there. A hyperactive or reactive dog is more likely to carry excess tension in their body than a dog at a normal energy level, because they simply don't know how to calm themselves down. Just as in humans, living with such a high level of stress can take its toll on the body. Massage therapy can help provide some relief to the body by helping to promote healthy circulation, as mentioned before, which helps not only the muscles, but also improves blood flow to the organs and brain.

Old or young, athlete or companion, healthy or suffering from injury or chronic conditions, all dogs stand to gain from the help of a qualified massage therapist. It's never too late for your dog to benefit from massage, and once they have you'll be asking yourself why you didn't start sooner.

Kristen McCartney is a certified animal massage therapist in Raeford, North Carolina. www.missbelles.com

Online Resources:

www.kenyoncanineinstitute
Kenyon Canine Institute
PO Pox 1701 Raeford NC 28376/ Phone 910-565-2154

www.missbelles.com
Miss Belle's® Etiquette School for Dogs
Raeford, North Carolina/ Phone 910-583-1924

www.kenyonk9foundation.org
Kenyon K9 Foundation™

www.deafdogsrocks.com
Deaf Dogs Rock

www.ttouch.com
Tellington Touch®

www.certifiedanimalbehaviorist.com
Certified Applied Animal Behaviorist

www.doggonesafe.com
Dog Bite Prevention

www.familypaws.com
Parent Education for Preparing Baby and Dog

www.cvillepetessentials.com
Holistic Pet Supplies

Resources for this Book:

Arizona Behavior Health Associates
http://psychotherapy.com/bio.html

Back Flowers
www.bachflowers.com

"Dominance in Domestic Dog—useful Construct or Bad Habit?" By John Bradshaw, Emily Blackwell, and Rachel Casey
http://www.journalvetbehavior.com/article/S1558-7878%2808%2900115-9

"Are you the Alpha Male?" http://www.huffingtonpost.com/tom-matlack/are-you-an-alpha-male_b_386519.html?

A Symphony in the Brain by Jim Robbins

Biofeedback for the Brain by Paul G. Swingle, Ph.D

Neurofeedback Transforming Your Life with Brain Biofeedback by Dr. Clare Albright

Control Unleashed by Leslie McDevitt

Control Unleashed The Puppy Program by Leslie McDevitt

The Other End of the Leash by Patricia McConnell

ADR The Animal Desk Reference Essential Oils for Animals by Melissa Shelton DVM

Clinical Behavioral Medicine for Small Animals By Dr. Karen Overall

"An Introduction to Biofeedback Tehnology and the Medical Science of Neurotherapy" by Kjell Sheldon Neilson

War Dogs by Michael G. Lemish

Other Good Reads & Resources:

Getting in TTouch with Your Puppy A Gentle Approach to Training and Influencing Behavior by Linda Tellington-Jones

Gotta Go! Successfully Potty Train Your Dog by Michelle Huntting

Whatever Happened to the Term Alpha Wolf? by Dr. L. David Mech

Dogs Are Gifts from God by Karen Palmer

Plenty in Life is Free by Kathy Sdao

Do as I Do! by Claudia Fugazza

Family Companion Dog by Renea Dahms

Additional Training for Impulse Control & Focus:

"Crate Games for Self-Control and Motivation" DVD by Susan Garrett

Learn More About Dog Body Language:

"The Language of Dogs Understanding Canine Body Language and Other Communication Signals" DVD by Sarah Kalnajs

MICHELLE HUNTTING

Join on-line group classes
Skype® sessions/phone consults

Miss Belle's®
PO Box 1701
Raeford, NC 28376

Phone: 910-583-1924

Email: info@missbelles.com

Follow Michelle Huntting:
www.michellehuntting.com
www.blogtalkradio.com/dogtalk
www.facebook.com/missbellesschoolfordogs

Made in the USA
Charleston, SC
27 September 2014